"*Living Joy* is an urgently needed message for a world grasping for joy but settling for short-lived pleasures. With his characteristic humor and insights from daily living the faith, Chris Stefanick shares the path to joy found by people who live in places as different as New Jersey and the slums of Haiti. *Living Joy* will help you to discover the joy that only Jesus Christ can give. 'These things I have spoken to you, that my joy may be in you, and that your joy may be full' (Jn 15:11)."

ARCHBISHOP SAMUEL J. AQUILA
Archdiocese of Denver

"In *Living Joy*, Chris Stefanick does a remarkable job at leading the reader on a journey to encounter joy. There is no doubt in my mind that if you follow his advice and spend time with this book you will experience a deeper joy in your life that the world will not be able to take away."

FR. DAVE PIVONKA, TOR
President, Franciscan University of Steubenville

"Chris Stefanick powerfully convinces us that God made us for joy—and he shows us how to actually live it. We need this message more than ever, and Chris has simply made it possible for us to choose a new way where lasting joy *is possible!*"

MOTHER GLORIA THERESE, OCD
Superior General, Carmelite Sisters of the Most Sacred Heart of Los Angeles

"Watch any Chris Stefanick talk, video, or storytelling and the first thing you'll see is authentic, contagious, pure joy. *How does he do that, all the time?! It's like dynamite!* He wants you to know that *you* have that within yourself also, and no one or nothing can deprive you of it. What is it, how do we tap into it, or feel and express it all the time, even and especially in the bad times? First, joy is a godsend. So is this book. It answers those questions and takes you on a simple but truly life-changing journey, and you'll never be the same. Cherish the opportunity!"

SHEILA LIAUGMINAS
Journalist, Author, Broadcaster

LIVING

JOY

CHRIS STEFANICK

LIVING

9 RULES TO HELP YOU REDISCOVER
AND **LIVE JOY EVERY DAY**

EMMAUS
ROAD
PUBLISHING

Steubenville, Ohio
www.emmausroad.org

Emmaus Road Publishing
1468 Parkview Circle
Steubenville, Ohio 43952

Library of Congress Control Number: 2020947736
ISBN 978-1-64585-081-6 (hard cover) / 978-1-64585-082-3 (paperback) /
978-1-64585-083-0 (ebook)

Cover design by Patty Borgman
Interior layout by Emily Demary
Photo Credit: Marliese Carmona

Contents

Introduction

These things I have spoken to you, that my joy
may be in you, and that your joy may be full.
—John 15:11

MY DAD had a heart attack recently, right in front of me.
I don't care how old you are, you always see your father
as a symbol of strength and stability. It's crushing to see
that foundation shaken at its core. He almost collapsed
as I helped him up the stairs and to the car. I was praying as we raced to the hospital, "God, please don't let
my father die in the passenger seat."

I love the good people who work in emergency
rooms. One nurse's eyes lit up when we pulled in. "It's
life-saving time," he said. I appreciated his optimism
but didn't share it. My dad has a long history of heart
disease.

After some scans, the doctor entered the room to
update us. You always want a doctor to come in with
a smile, a plan, and a pill to make everything better.
But, every once in a while, the doctor comes in with a
grim face and unhappy news. If this hasn't happened
to you yet, it eventually will because, well, no one gets
out alive. (Sorry to break that news to you.) He shook

his head and said, "His arteries are just blocked every-where. There's nothing I can really do."

Through a string of small miracles and great doctors, my dad pulled through that day. But we were convinced that his road had come to an end. There was a weight in the air of the intensive care unit where I sat with him and my mother, his wife of forty-nine years, waiting for the inevitable. And in that darkness, the light of my parents' quiet heroism shone bright.

My mother looked at me and said, "I have no right to complain to God about anything. I'm grateful for the life we've been given. I'm grateful for these forty-nine years." I could see the deep pain in her eyes, but there was something deeper.

Then my dad spoke. He asked to hold my rosary, put it against his chest, grinned, and said, "I'm posing for my casket." Then he calmly said, "I'm not worried about a thing." I could see the deep pain in his chest, but there was something deeper.

It was joy. Real joy. Not the fake "joy" born of denial or wishful thinking. The pain was real, and we were facing it together. But the joy was "realer."

For the Christian:

- Joy isn't what happens when life goes perfectly. It's what happens when you know you're loved perfectly, even when life's a mess.
- Joy isn't winning. It's when you know you've already won.
- Joy isn't an absence of pain. It's the presence of Jesus.

This book is about claiming the joy you were created for. It's a joy you can have right now, even if you're sitting in an ICU, because it doesn't depend on a change in your circumstances; rather, it depends on a change in you.

And what excites me the most about this project is that I'm going to show you exactly how to get it. But you have work to do. Let's begin.

Got Joy?

*Your hearts will rejoice, and no one will take
your joy from you.* —*John 16:22*

JOY ISN'T A LUXURY. It's a necessity. Every human heart
is born looking for it. And every heart is powered by it.

THE ATTRACTION OF JOY

You. Want. Joy.

You want *real* happiness, not just a passing "good
mood." And your desire for joy is driving everything
else you've ever looked for in life. In fact, we only want
other things because we all want that *one thing*. If you're
looking for money, it's because you think money will
give you joy. If you want success, it's because you think
success will give you joy. If you want to make an impact
in the world, if you want your kids to be stable, if you
want a great marriage, or if you want a yacht docked on
Kauai with your own personal bartender to mix your
martinis (I hope you get that, and I hope that you invite

me over), it's all for one reason. You want to be happy. You want joy.

How did I know that? Because I'm a mind reader. And we all have basically the same "stuff" between our ears. The human brain hasn't changed much for a few hundred thousand years. And the human spirit hasn't veered from that one longing since we carved our dreams of happy hunts on cave walls and left our handprints for future generations—united in the same longing across time—to find. (High five, caveman.)

> "Circumstances may break a man's bones, but not his joy."
> —Ryan Lovett

We're all looking for joy.[1] And that longing cuts across ages, cultures, and religions. Aristotle taught that happiness is the end—the "telos"—behind everything we do. The Dalai Lama said, "We 7 billion human beings—emotionally, mentally, physically—are the same. Everyone wants a joyful life."[2] St. Pope John Paul II, when he was eighty-two years old, talking to hundreds of thousands of young people in Toronto, reached across generations with the words, "Dear young people . . . I have felt the deep longing that beats within your hearts: *you want to be happy!*"[3]

---

[1] I'll use the words happiness and joy interchangeably, but with a preference for joy. Happiness has come to imply a contentedness based on circumstances. Joy is something eternal. And, since our hearts are made for heaven, small doses of a happiness based on happenstance won't do. Joy more closely captures what you're looking for.

[2] Charlie Campbell, "The Dalai Lama Has Been the Face of Buddhism for 60 Years. China Wants to Change That," *Time*, March 7, 2019, https://time.com/longform/dalai-lama-60-year-exile/.

[3] John Paul II, Address by the Holy Father John Paul II, July 25, 2002,

In the words of Blaise Pascal, "All men seek happiness. This is without exception. . . . The cause of some going to war, and of others avoiding it, is the same desire in both with different views. This is the motive of every action of every man, even of those who hang themselves."[4] That's an extreme thing to ponder, that even when a man does something as misguided and tragic as putting his head in a noose, what he *really* wants is to escape pain *so that* he can find happiness.[5]

We're all looking for joy. Unmovable, heavenly, eternal joy. Not when we're dead. Now. Joy *is* success. Accomplishment without joy is total failure.

And not only does joy give meaning to every milestone; joy gives you the strength to build the life you were made for as you strive to hit those milestones. That's right: joy is power.

THE POWER OF JOY

Everyone pulls their strength from somewhere. Many are driven by powerful emotions like anger, lust, or pride; others are driven by the promise of power, money, or fame. But the greatest and most tenacious driver in life is joy. Joy isn't just the feeling of contentedness that comes from the fight being over. It's the strength to enter the

http://www.vatican.va/content/john-paul-ii/en/speeches/2002/july/documents/hf_jp-ii_spe_20020725_wyd-address-youth.html.

[4] Blaise Pascal, *Pensées*, trans. W. F. Trotter (Mineola, NY: Dover Publications, 2018), no. 425.

[5] There's a similar launch to my book *The Search*, written with Paul McCusker, which focuses entirely on Rule 9 in this book! So, if you're not convinced of that rule when you reach the end, pick up *The Search*.

fight in the first place. If your life is a car, joy is the gas. If your life is a battle, joy is your sword and shield.

In the fifth century BC, the Jewish people were scattered and tired. Jews living in exile in Persia learned that their city walls in Jerusalem had been torn down. City walls were a big deal back then. There were no international peace treaties to protect you. There were no smartphones and social media to publicize human rights violations. If your neighbors wanted to take your land and you had no walls, they took it and killed your family in the process. In addition to Jerusalem having no walls, four neighboring nations (that they knew of) wanted them dead.

Nehemiah led the charge to leave the safety of exile and go home to rebuild their city—to risk everything to claim the lives they were made for. As exciting as that is, it must have sounded to the Jewish people like an invitation to a pool party with a school of sharks.

So, Nehemiah gathered them together—knowing many of them might die for the cause, and he said, "The joy of the Lord is your strength" (Neh 8:10).

I can almost hear the murmuring crowd: "Who could talk about joy at a time like this? Is this guy crazy?" But, just like when my dad was at death's door, joy is precisely what they needed. (And like most prophets, he probably was just a little bit crazy, but in a good way.)

You don't get joy after the battle is won. You need the power of joy to enter the battle: the big battles, and the battle of everyday life.

I'm a fan of boxing. Some of the greatest boxers in history smiled as they entered the ring. Not the smug

"I'm gonna beat you" smile, but the Manny Pacquiao, "I'm a kid about to have a lot of fun playing my favorite sport right now" kind of smile. He probably had the same smile as he helped save his family from starvation by subsistence fishing as a young boy in the Philippines. It's stunning how not angry he looked as he won title after title in an incredibly violent sport. I think that joy fueled his rise from dire poverty to being one of the world's wealthiest men.

When you live a life fueled by joy, *you* become an unstoppable force.

So, how is joy power, exactly?

- It makes temptations easy to topple. You simply prefer the spiritual joy over the promise of passing pleasure.
- It makes forgiving people easier. Why? Because that person may have taken something from you, but you didn't let them take the one thing that mattered.
- Joy makes it easy to pursue dreams, because inevitable failures can't crush a joyful person.
- Joy makes you a natural leader and faith sharer, because it makes you magnetic and attractive, and people want to follow your lead when they are around you.
- Joy makes your setbacks setups for comebacks. It gives you the right perspective to face every challenge in your life.
- Joy even helps you get more done at work. "In fact, one meta-analysis of over 275,000 people across more than 200 studies found that happy people

aren't just more productive—they also receive higher evaluations for quality of work, dependability, and creativity. Another study found that students who are more cheerful in college were more financially successful than their peers over a decade after graduation."[6]

- Joy even impacts your physical health. Harvard conducted an unprecedented study, which tracked 268 students over the course of 75 years to find out what factors would make them happy, successful, and healthy in their old age. I'll share more about what they discovered later, but for now, the article that summed up the research was entitled "Good Genes Are Nice, But Joy Is Better."[7] They even found that if someone was joyful in their fifties, that was a better predictor than cholesterol of whether they'd be alive and happy at eighty. So, fire up the grill and eat up those bacon-covered burgers, friends! (In moderation, of course . . . if that makes you happy.)

- Finally, joy makes you a force for good in the world. In the words of then-Cardinal Ratzinger (later Pope Benedict XVI), "The deepest poverty is the inability of joy, the tediousness of a life considered absurd and contradictory . . . The inability of joy presupposes and produces the inability to love, produces jealousy, avarice—all defects that devas-

---

[6] Brendon Burchard, *High Performance Habits: How Extraordinary People Become That Way* (Carlsbad, CA: Hay House, 2017), 178.

[7] Liz Mineo, "Good Genes Are Nice, But Joy Is Better," *The Harvard Gazette*, April 11, 2017, https://news.harvard.edu/gazette/story/2017/04/over-nearly-80-years-harvard-study-has-been-showing-how-to-live-a-healthy-and-happy-life/.

tate the life of individuals and of the world."[8]

Simply put, misery is contagious and, if unchecked, ultimately leads to war. Joy is equally contagious and leads to a better world . . . the kind that contented people naturally create.

Given all of the above, we can't afford to be passive recipients of our passing moods, driven through life by how we "feel" in the moment. There's an absolute urgency to work on your joy. Joy is strength. Joy *must be* your strength.

The devil also knows that joy is strength, and he wants you to be weak. That's why so many of the battles in the spiritual life, if you pay attention, are simply the devil trying to rob you of your joy. You need to know exactly how to win that daily battle because your family, coworkers, church, friends, and the world need you to!

> "Joy is the simplest form of gratitude."
> —Karl Barth

MORE THAN A FEELING

As you can tell by now, when I use the word "joy," I'm not talking about a "surface-y" experience. Deeper joy—spiritual joy—is a serious thing. Like the depths of the ocean, it's unmoved by the surface chop. Spiritual joy can exist deep within us even when the surface is battered by the storms of sadness, struggles, and failures.

---

[8] Quoted in Stephen Mansfield, *Pope Benedict XVI: His Life and Mission* (New York: Penguin, 2005), 170.

And that's when we need it most.

This book isn't about your surface feelings. It's okay to not feel happy all the time. It's okay to be up at night with anxiety. It's okay to feel frustrated. Because it's okay to be human. If you read this with the skewed idea that to "succeed spiritually" you need to feel happy all the time, you'll only end up tweaked out and over-examining your feelings all the time. That's not the goal of the spiritual life. In fact, if you're overly focused on your feelings, you'll end up miserable. Ironic, eh?

Your feelings are born of chemical concoctions in your brain. Your spiritual dispositions (which sometimes lead to deep feelings and sometimes don't) come from your soul. And you can experience both at the same time. Have you ever felt deeply sad and hopeful at the same time? It's what we experience at funerals where we both say goodbye and remember heaven. The sadness you feel at a funeral is natural and normal. It's a neurological response to "goodbye." The hope you feel is happening someplace deeper inside of you. It's a spiritual response to the faith that the goodbye you're experiencing is just "goodbye for now." You can't always control the natural biology within you any more than you can control nature outside of you, and that's why feelings, as important as they are, need to be put in their place. The spiritual movement toward joy can and will bubble up to happy feelings. But feelings rise and fall like the tide. Our goal is something deeper than that. It's to work for a constant spiritual disposition of joy, of receptivity to and of delight in reality and eventually the Ultimate Reality: God.

Three Disclaimers:

1. You need to *meta* your *noia*.

Before we embark on the rules for a more joyful life, I need to drop a bomb on you. The way you're going to get the life you're looking for boils down to one word: REPENT!

That sounds like a pretty negative way to start a book on joy, doesn't it? But it's how Jesus started his public ministry. In three of the four Gospels, Jesus kicked it all off by shouting out the word "repent" to the world. He later said, "These things I have spoken to you, that my joy may be in you, and that your joy may be full" (John 15:11). In other words, everything he taught humanity was so that we'd experience the joy of God. (That's a LOT of superhuman joy.) That means that the word "repent" is the starting gate to a race that ends in joy.

Huh? How?

Well, you have to look at what the word Jesus used *actually* means. The New Testament was written in Greek. And the word that's commonly translated as "repent" is *metanoia*, and that literally means "to change your thinking." *Meta* (change) your *noia* (thinking).

So, the bomb that just dropped on you is this: your lack of joy, and the ways you don't feel like you're living the life you were made for, isn't because of your circumstances. It's because of you. The biggest obstacle between you and joy is yourself.

All too often, we blame our circumstances:

- I'll be peaceful *when* my teenager starts respecting me. (Don't hold your breath.)
- I'll be confident *when* I'm CEO.
- I'll be happy *when* my wife starts treating me right and I make enough money.
- I'll be focused on what matters most *when* life calms down in the month of Septober (the month that never comes).

No. You'll be a joyful person when *you* change. That's bad news because it's hard. It's good news because that's the one thing in your life you *do* have some degree of control over.

2. This book is simple.

This book spells out nine rules to help you claim the joy and the life you were made for. And they're all simple. Some might say "stupidly simple." (I prefer brilliantly simple!) Anyone can overcomplicate things. You do it to yourself all the time. So do I. Simplicity takes hard work. But the difference between an amazing life and an okay life is whether or not we actually stick to those stupidly simple things that we *know* make life amazing.

This book isn't meant to burden you with complex and time-consuming solutions. These are all small changes. But if you've ever shot a rifle, you know that a very small change in your direction has a radical impact on your destination. If a target is two hundred yards away and you shift your aim a few inches, you'll miss it altogether.

If you start living by these simple rules, you'll hit

your mark over the course of your life. If you don't, you'll miss it.

After reading this book, you might come up with twenty more rules. Don't write to me that I left out X. Have at it. Write the sequel! This isn't a definitive or exhaustive list. It's just what I've found works for me. It's also all based on the ancient wisdom of Scripture, a lot of cutting-edge research, and proven impact. I've carried this message in my years of traveling, speaking, and coaching a million people around the world. If it works for the countless people I've been blessed to help, it will work for you too.

> "Ask, and you will receive, that your joy may be full."
> —John 16:24

3. This book is based on evidence, experience, and common sense.

This book is based on research and, as you'll see, a lot of hard-to-refute, real-life experience that will resonate with you as true. Let me tell you what doesn't resonate as true and what I've intentionally left out of my research: all the studies done on "the world's happiest countries."

How could I leave out something so glaringly important in a book about joy? Because the studies are wrong. Anyone who's actually read the studies knows they're not about *real* joy. National happiness ratings include things like "sustainability." Don't get me wrong, I think recycling is important. I just don't mistake being green for being truly happy inside. I don't think you do either. They also rate wealth as a happiness indicator.

Again, that's not unimportant, but we've all encountered wealthy people who are miserable. (The reason why is in Rule 8.)

I've been all around the world. I can tell you that there are far fewer smiles in the wealthy and beautiful city of Prague than in Duverger, Haiti, where "smile" is an understatement for the inner light that wells up and shines on the people's faces there. (I'll tell you their secret in Rule 1.)

You Can Get There from Here

Rise, let us go from here. —*John 14:31*

Listen, it doesn't matter where you're starting from. I don't care if you feel like your life is in shambles. God believes in you, and so do I. All that matters is that you begin the journey toward joy. If you do that, you can and will hit the target of *your better life*.

You may have heard the joke about the guy who asked for directions and was told, "You can't get there from here." That's funny because it's never true. You can get to any point B from literally any point A on earth. Your location is not an obstacle to where God wants to bring you if you start changing your direction now. You can always begin to live the life you were made for. Your current location does not impact your destination.

On a personal note, I'm so passionate to take this journey with you because of what I've *seen* these nine rules do for me and for so many others. Shifting my focus from the complex issues of everyday life to following these simple rules has changed my life, and, ironically, has helped me tackle all the issues life throws at me more effectively too. Your problems might be complicated. This book isn't about your problems. Just simple solutions.

In short: These nine rules have changed my life for the better. They'll change yours too.

HOW TO USE THIS BOOK

I don't recommend reading this book straight through. There's just too much here. I want this book to change your life, so take your time with it! Journal. Jot down notes for exactly how you plan to live out each rule.

Finally, there is a How-To section at the end of every rule (except for Rule 4, which is self-explanatory). I'd encourage you to go through this book with friends and connect every week, even for short phone call, to discuss your progress.

We remember what we read far more when we write it down, and even more when we then talk about it with others. So be sure to read, journal, and share.

Let's begin.

Rule 1: Give Thanks

Give thanks in all circumstances; for this is the will of God in Christ Jesus for you.
—1 Thessalonians 5:18

OUR FIRST RULE is so powerful that I considered writing a whole book just on this. It's also so simple that most people overlook its power in their lives and forget to be intentional about it. It's gratitude. Giving thanks. But as simple as it is, it doesn't come naturally. This book will show you how. And when you implement this rule in your daily life, your life and your attitude *will* change for the better.

IT COULDN'T POSSIBLY BE THIS SIMPLE. OR COULD IT?

A lot of people wonder what the secret sauce for a happy

life is, and why God doesn't just tell us. Turns out he did, but what he said is simple, and we're busy looking for a mystic light to shine from behind a cloud—illuminating a hidden path. We're looking for a guru to teach us secret spiritual methods that the "average" person couldn't possibly understand.

People have fallen into this error throughout history. We overlook the simple solutions hiding right under our noses.

When Naaman, a great army commander, got leprosy, he was horrified. It was a death sentence in the ancient world. And a painful one. But a ray of hope broke through when he learned of a great prophet in Israel. A mystic. A spiritual man. He went on a long journey to find Elisha and beg for healing. When he found Elisha, he was waiting for some powerful ceremony. Or perhaps he'd be told to climb to the highest cliff and eat the egg of a rare bird nesting in the rocks. Or at least some spell would be cast in a strange language. But Elisha told him bathe seven times in the Jordan, and he'd be healed. Then the prophet walked off . . . like a regular, boring old guy.

> "It's 'heaven begun' for the grateful on earth."
> —Solanus Casey

"The prophet was obviously wrong. It can't be this stupidly simple. I've made a long journey to a great spiritual man, and he's telling me to take a bath!?" Naaman stormed off in a rage. One of Naaman's servants stopped him. "If the prophet had commanded you to do some great thing, would you not have done it? How much rather, then, when he says to you, 'Wash, and be clean'?" (2 Kgs 5:13).

Naaman relented. He had come all this way. Nothing to lose, he thought. He did as the prophet told him, and as Scripture says, his skin became "like the flesh of a little child" (2 Kgs 5:14).

Do you want your youth restored? Your marriage healed? Blessings to be unleashed in your life? Your mood improved? Your house happier? Do you want to get more out of your life? It's simpler than you think: "Give thanks in all circumstances; for this is the will of God in Christ Jesus for you" (1 Thess 5:18).

THE POWER OF GRATITUDE

Gratitude is POWERFUL.

Gratitude:

- Makes it possible for you to enjoy the blessings you have.
- Strengthens relationships, because when people feel appreciated by you, they want to be around you.
- Sets you up for promotion from people above you and loyalty from people who work for you, because everyone wants to bless those who are grateful for it.
- Releases oxytocin and dopamine in the brain, the all-natural "feel-good" chemicals.
- Makes you a blessing magnet. In the words of St. Therese of Lisieux, "What most attracts God's graces is gratitude, because if we thank him for

a gift, he is touched and hastens to give us ten more, and if we thank him again with the same enthusiasm, what an incalculable multiplication of graces! I have experienced this; try it yourself and you will see! My gratitude for everything he gives me is limitless, and I prove it to him in a thousand ways."[1]

To the contrary, ingratitude is poison that robs you of the life you were made for.

Ingratitude:

- Blocks the blessings of almighty God.
- Keeps you from enjoying the blessings you have.
- Destroys friendships.
- Kills marriages. I've literally seen marriages end because one or both of the spouses let in a stream of toxic, ungrateful thoughts. (If you start looking for the flaws in your spouse instead of the gifts, trust me, you'll find them. And look out: they'll find the flaws in you!)
- Makes people not want to bless or promote you, because who wants to bless an ingrate?
- Ruins your mood and robs your joy.

In the words of Solanus Casey, "Be sure, if the enemy of our souls is pleased at anything in us it is ingratitude—of whatever kind. Why? Ingratitude leads to so many breaks with God and neighbor." He also said that "gratitude is as necessary for social order and harmony as are the laws of gravity for the physical world."

---

[1] Jacques Philippe, *The Way of Trust and Love: A Retreat Guided by St. Thérèse of Lisieux* (New York: Scepter Publishers, 2001), 111.

It Doesn't Come Naturally

But gratitude, as important and simple as it is, doesn't come naturally. We're all-natural malcontents. None of us come into this world happy. We come into the world kicking and screaming. That's our default. And there's a reason for that.

Let's blame it on the cavemen. The human brain hasn't changed much since we wrote on cave walls. And the brain, like our other organs, didn't form to make us happy. It formed to keep us alive. The caveman who was good at stopping and smelling the roses was probably not good at surviving. You didn't get his genes because they were eaten by a saber-toothed tiger while he was enjoying a nice sunset and sipping a glass of whatever cavemen used to drink. It's the one who obsessed about what might hurt him that survived long enough to pass his genes on to you.

Fast-forward forty thousand years from your great-grandpa to the tenth power who survived because he was always watching his back, and you walk through life watching your back. You're driving through traffic. Someone cuts you off. You spend the rest of the drive looking for that guy. You might even think about him all night.

You've never come home after a hard day of work and traffic and said, "That was rough. And I just can't stop thinking about that one nice guy who let me in front of him in traffic. I'm trying to focus on the kids, but all I can think of is his smiling face as he waved at me." No. You spend the rest of the day thinking about the one jerk who cut you off. You obsess. You almost revel in your own annoyance. You only get about thirty thousand days to live. How many days have you wasted thinking about the one jerk you encountered that day?

It's human nature, I guess.

It's also human nature to bond together over what annoys us. How many gatherings land on a discussion about the problems in the world? How many church meetings home in on the problems with your pastor? How many connections around the watercooler at work land on complaining about the boss? We get to-gether and "tribalize" against what bigger force might hurt us. It's a caveman survival mechanism. Again, it's natural.

Aren't you tired of living in the natural? St. Paul shows us how to rise above it.

PAUL'S SECRET SAUCE

St. Paul was an adventurer. A leader. A man who called the shots. And he was naturally drawn to all those things. When the first Christian, Stephen, was killed for his faith, his executioners laid their cloaks at the feet of Saul (Paul's old name). He was in charge.

And he couldn't stay put. He journeyed from place to place to find more and more Christians to persecute. His life was spent on the road.

His conversion happened on the road to Damascus, and God met him on the move—because he was always on the move.

And, after his conversion, he applied that same

adventurous spirit, previously given over to hatred, to spreading the love of Jesus Christ. Go! Go! Go! He spent his ministry ever on the road to somewhere.

Some estimates say he traveled over ten thousand miles during his public ministry. That's almost the width of the United States four times. That's easy if you have Southwest Airlines. With that much travel, he may have even gotten special airline status, boarded first, and enjoyed first class for most of his trips! Not so much two thousand years ago. To travel back then was to risk death every time.

This is the way he describes it:

> Three times I have been beaten with rods; once I was stoned. Three times I have been ship-wrecked; a night and a day I have been adrift at sea; on frequent journeys, in danger from rivers, danger from robbers, danger from my own people, danger from Gentiles, danger in the city, danger in the wilderness, danger at sea, danger from false brethren; in toil and hardship, through many a sleepless night, in hunger and thirst, often without food, in cold and exposure. (2 Cor 11:25–27)

But you know what? I don't think any of that bothered him much. Brushes with death put a glimmer in his eye. I think 2 Corinthians 11 was some manly bragging! He was the Navy Seal of the early Church.

I think the real struggle for this road warrior came when he was clamped in chains and had to spend two years under house arrest. Bored. No more journeys. No more death-defying experiences. No more seeing the faces he loved. No more watching the light go on in someone's eyes as they heard the Gospel for the first time.

However, it was there that he did some of his most important work. Much of what he wrote to the world—and perhaps most importantly, much of what he wrote about joy—was from prison.

From prison, hidden from the world, cut off from a life of adventure, awaiting his beheading, he wrote, "I have learned, in whatever state I am, to be content" (Phil 4:11). I'm not sure I'd take that too seriously if he had written it from a beach in Cancún. Anyone can be content in a lounge chair. He wrote that from prison. But that didn't come naturally for Paul, just like it doesn't come naturally for you. He had to work hard at it. And so do we.

And from prison he outlines how: through gratitude, praise, and worship.

From prison, he wrote to the Philippians, "Rejoice in the Lord always; again I will say, Rejoice" (Phil 4:4). That was a command! My mom used to tell me, "Joy is a choice, Christopher." She was right.

Paul continues, joy dripping from his pen, "Have no anxiety about anything, but in everything by prayer and supplication with thanksgiving let your requests be made known to God. And the peace of God, which passes all understanding, will keep your hearts and your minds in Christ Jesus" (Phil 4:6–7).

Pay attention to what he said, "in everything . . . *with thanksgiving*." Every prayer and thought, even when we give voice to the things we need, should be covered in thanksgiving.

The Eucharist has been the center of Christian worship since day one of the Church. The word "Eucharist" means "thanks." Is thanks at the center of your prayer? Is it at the center of your soul?

If it isn't, you're doing it wrong. And you're bound to be miserable, even if you pray a lot. But if it is, even when life gets hard, you're bound to be joyful. And more, you're bound to be unstoppable.

You couldn't conquer Paul, and he knew it. He wrote, "We are more than conquerors" (Rom 8:37). In other words, "Conqueror is an understatement for what we are!"

Every struggle thrown at Paul was turned on its head:

- You couldn't murder Paul, but you could make him a martyr.
- You couldn't imprison Paul, but you could shift his ministry from traveling evangelist to writer.
- You couldn't offend Paul, but you could give him an opportunity to forgive.
- You couldn't starve Paul, but you could help him fast better.
- You couldn't put Paul on trial, but you could give him a pulpit to preach from before the world's judges.

Paul was more than a conqueror. Are you? If not, try giving thanks more.

HAITI'S SECRET SAUCE

I got a glimpse of the light of St. Paul's unconquerable spirit when I went to Haiti. My interest in Haiti began when I picked up my little girl from school a few years ago. She said, "Dad, I had a miserable day." She's ten years old, perfectly healthy, and well-fed. She lives in a prosperous nation. How truly miserable could school have been? I wanted to give her a dose of perspective. This is probably not the healthiest thing to do, but then again, I'm not a licensed psychologist. So, I googled pictures of kids in Haiti. I wanted to show her that many kids around the world *actually* struggled today just to survive. All I could find were pictures of kids smiling.

"The person who is filled with gratitude toward God, whose life is permeated by this primary attitude of gratitude, is also the only person who is truly awake."
—Dieterich von Hildebrand

I went on a mission trip to Haiti not long after that. The kids in Haiti smile more than kids in Disneyland. Not to downplay the suffering there, but when they smile, it's more like an inner light welling up from the depths than a smile. I've heard the phrase "Her smile could light up a room." That's rarely a true statement, except in Haiti. I saw countless smiles like that.

They've got nothing compared with what you've been blessed with, but they do have a lot of gratitude. They are constantly thanking God. They are constantly thanking each other. Nothing they have is overlooked. Gratitude is the key that will unlock the smile on your face.

They bring that gratitude to church with them. When I got to preach in Haiti, I was nervous when no one showed up for my 5 p.m. presentation. I went to my friend who organized the event and asked where everyone was. He laughed and said, "5 p.m. doesn't mean anything in a town where no one owns a watch. They'll eventually come." Of course, the church filled up two hours later. They were in no rush to come. But what really blew me away was how they were in no rush to leave. No one left after my talk, which was followed by a long Mass, which was followed by an hour of praise and worship, which was followed by some of the most joyous dancing I'd ever seen. Young and old became like little kids. Hands in the air. Huge smiles. Celebrating life, faith, and family. They all looked like they had just won the super lotto. And they had nothing.

When you ask a Haitian, "How are you?" the typical response is "Strong." Gratitude leads to joy, and joy makes us strong. Haitians don't tend to focus on what gets them down. They focus on what they have to do today and on being grateful for the things that do go well in their lives. Poverty, earthquakes, political instability, hurricanes knocking out what few crops they successfully grow, are all met by them getting up the next day and going to work again and giving thanks for what they have.

After the earthquake that claimed hundreds of thousands of lives in 2010, the people gathered in the capital with drums and started beating them out loud, many of them praising God as they did so. They wanted to show the world that they could shake the earth too. They're amazing people. They will build an amazing nation some day because of it.

Listen, I didn't want to downplay my fourth grader's "first-world problems"; I certainly don't want to downplay the problems in Haiti, and I also don't want to downplay yours. And maybe as you read this you're thinking, "But Chris, my problems are real! Giving thanks more won't make them go away!"

I'm sure they are real. But you know what else is real? The sun. When you go for a walk, do you stare at it? If you do, it will zap-fry your retinas. Look at the flowers instead. You can't control what's around you, but you can control what's within you. You can control what you focus on and let into your heart.

The end result of Paul's advice to give praise, written from chains, is where it focused his heart from that dark place and where it will lift ours. "Finally, brethren, whatever is true, whatever is honorable, whatever is just, whatever is pure, whatever is lovely, whatever is gracious, if there is any excellence, if there is anything worthy of praise, think about these things" (Phil 4:8).

Many Haitians aren't brought low by their circumstances. Are you? If so, try giving thanks more.

ANNE FRANK'S SECRET SAUCE

Before we dive into how to become more grateful, I want to hold up one more example to encourage you: Anne Frank.

Pictures of Anne have always cut me to the heart—her preteen smile, that gleam in her eye in the midst of a world going up in flames. Anne was a giant of a human being, not because she did anything momentous but because she simply stayed who she was despite the profound evil that set the stage for her brief life. That power had everything to do with where she fixed her attention—it had everything to do with gratitude.

When Anne was four years old, her family had to flee Nazi Germany for the Netherlands. When she was ten, the Nazis clamped down on the Netherlands and cut Jews off from parks, theaters, and work. At thirteen, after a failed attempt to leave for the United States, her family joined another family in a cramped attic where they hid for two years. At fifteen, the Nazis raided their Secret Annex. Her family was separated when they were sent to Auschwitz to do hard labor. She and her mother would never see her father again. She was eventually transferred to another disease-infested camp where she and her mother died of typhoid.

When she was in hiding, Anne wrote, "Think of all the beauty in yourself and in everything around you and be happy." And perhaps her most famous quote, "I still believe, in spite of everything, that people are truly good at heart."[2]

She was able to find beauty in that attic. She was able to find goodness in her fellow man. Her young eyes peered through the dark night and found glimmers

---

[2] Anne Frank, *The Diary of a Young Girl*, ed. Otto H. Frank and Mirjam Pressler, trans. Susan Massotty (New York: Doubleday, 2001), 211, 333.

of light and things to be grateful for. What do you see when you look at the events of your life?

Do you see the people who hurt you? Or the news feed (which I don't recommend looking at too often)? Or the bad roll of the dice that hurt your portfolio? Or the bully who cut you down in middle school twenty years ago? Or the parents who tried hard but didn't love you quite the way you needed?

Or do your eyes peer through the darkness in your life to find something more? Gratitude will help you see the *something more.* It will help you find the beauty and goodness.

Gratitude might not change your circumstances, but it does change you. It gives you the capacity to have a gleam in your eye even if your world is going up in flames.

Anne was able to find things to delight in even when life was very hard. Are you? If not, try giving thanks more.

THE KEY TO ENJOYING LIFE IS . . . YOU GUESSED IT!

Gratitude isn't just the key to having the unconquerable spirit of St. Paul, my heroes in Haiti, or Anne Frank; on a much simpler level, it's also the key to enjoying your everyday life.

If you don't have gratitude, God is wasting his blessings on you. Some of the harshest words in Scripture aren't addressed to the murderer or adulterer but to the ungrateful—the man covered in blessings who can't seem to enjoy them. "A man may have a hundred children and live many years; yet no matter how long he lives, if he cannot enjoy his prosperity . . . I say that a stillborn child is better off than he. It comes without meaning . . ." (Eccl 6:3–4, NIV). Did you catch that? You'd be better off if you were born dead than if you have blessings but don't stop and enjoy them. Ouch. That's harsh.

But isn't that you sometimes? Half of your daily stress comes from complaining about juggling your many blessings—your children, managing your home, scheduling time with family and friends. You wouldn't have to do any of those things if you didn't have money, kids, or freedom of religion.

I fall into the error of stressing over my blessings all the time! I'm still learning with you. I went paddle boarding with my family recently. I had a moment of "misery." The AC in my car broke. I was sweating by the time I got to the lake. The pump for my inflatable paddleboard broke so I had to do it by hand. More sweat. I was cursing the universe by the time I had the board pumped up. I was a stressed-out mess. Then I stopped, took a deep breath, and reflected on my circumstances with new eyes. I was at a beautiful national park in Colorado near where I live. I actually had the money to buy a couple of paddleboards. I have healthy children whose bodies are able to paddleboard. My car AC had apparently broken, but I have a car. I began to thank God. That didn't fix my AC or my paddleboard pump, but it did fix me.

"Every man also to whom God has given wealth

and possessions and power to enjoy them, and to accept his lot and find enjoyment in his toil [note that the Scripture doesn't overlook the fact that life has plenty of toil!]—this is the gift of God. For he will not much remember the days of his life because God keeps him occupied with joy in his heart" (Eccl 5:19–20).

Do you want to be occupied with joy in your heart? Give thanks.

How-To

Ideals don't mean much unless they become practicals. That's why every rule for living joy will end with a How-To section. I'm going to give you three practicals that will make you a grateful person, and I want you to stick to them every day. And they're simple. Nothing in this book is meant to take a lot of time or complicate your life. But if you want your life to change for the better, you have to stick to them.

1. Count your "gratefuls" every morning.

Every day when I wake up, my body starts to do its job: keep Chris alive. Cortisol increases, turning on energy like a switch. Insulin kicks in, making me ready to eat. Aldosterone drops, which takes me to the toilet so I'm ready to run. Testosterone spikes, making me ready to fight every battle that might come my way the second I wake up. Caveman Chris is ready! The body is an amazing "survival machine."

And as this chemical firework show goes off in my

body, my brain kicks into overdrive, jumping into all the challenges I might face in a given day. That's what it does. It's a problem-solving machine. It dives into every problem, anticipates every threat, and tackles every to-do before my feet hit the floor.

Ever notice that when you wake up too early, it's hard to get back to sleep? Every system in your caveman body is lining up to get you moving, running from the saber-toothed tiger, seeking out the next watering hole, and spearing the next squirrel to feed your family.

But your natural systems aren't the boss of you. "If anyone is in Christ, he is a new creation" (2 Cor 5:17). We're more than natural creatures, driven by natural processes.

So, here's what I do every day when I wake up, and I want you to do the same thing. When my brain first wakes up, before my eyes open, I begin to direct my thoughts away from my problems, my to-do list, the news feed, and toward my "gratefuls." I take captive every thought and make it obedient to Christ (see 2 Cor 10:5). I begin to give thanks. My prayer isn't eloquent at that pre-coffee hour.

"Thank you, Lord, for the blue of the sky, the breath I just took, the work I'll get to do, another day to serve you and others, the little feet that are already running down the hall to interrupt my prayer . . . because they won't be doing that for long. Thank you."

That simple act of gratitude reorients my mind from stressed to blessed, from homing in on dark things to "whatever is lovely, whatever is gracious . . ." (Phil 4:8).

And I hit the ground ready to be a joy to those around me rather than a drain.

2. Let trials "trigger" your gratitude.

Job is the oldest book of the Bible. Maybe that's because suffering is the oldest challenge to faith mankind has ever faced. Job had what one might call a "terrible, horrible, no good, very bad day." In a single day, he lost his sons and daughters, servants, and livestock. Then he was afflicted with bodily sores. And then all his friends started to gossip about him. There is a book's worth of reflections we can dive into about Job and the problem of pain, but let's save that for another book. For now, I want to home in on Job's first response to it all.

Right at the start of the book, his response to the worst day ever was praise. "Job arose, and tore his robe, and shaved his head [a sign of mourning], and fell upon the ground, and worshiped" (Job 1:20). He praised God for his greatness. He thanked God for his life. "Naked I came from my mother's womb, and naked shall I return; the Lord gave, and the Lord has taken away; blessed be the name of the Lord" (Job 1:21). In other words, "God doesn't owe me anything, so everything above zero, including just getting to exist, is an occasion for gratitude from a non-necessary creature such as me." But it wasn't just holy for Job to give thanks; it was necessary for his life to go on. You see, the Book of Job ends with countless blessings and opportunities being heaped back upon him. He wouldn't have had the strength to rise up from the ashes and grab those blessings, or the heart to enjoy them, if he decided to close up shop in Job 1.

I met a young woman at an event recently. She appeared perfectly healthy but struggled intensely. She'd had a Job incident, and it was crushing her spirit. She had been in a car accident and suffered from a traumatic brain injury. In addition to problems concentrating and sleeping, she needed daily physical therapy for a multitude of ailments from the accident. She approached me with her mother at her side, and they both asked, "Why did God let this happen?" I'd usually respond with the theological answer to that question, about how a loving God could let people he loves suffer, and how that's not a sign that he's abandoned us. But I felt inspired to go a different route because I could tell that wasn't going to help. I answered her question with the question, "Is that question helping you?"

It caught her off guard. So, I pressed further: "Seriously, what's that doing for you to keep asking that every day? You have the struggle of daily physical therapy, and you're going to add to that struggle by focusing on exhausting questions about the existential meaning of suffering? Stop it."

I could see a weight lifted off her shoulders. We *think* we need every question answered. Our brains tell us we do. We don't. I refocused her on her blessings. "This accident didn't happen *to* you. It happened *for* you. Look at how compassionate this struggle has made you toward others. Look at your beautiful eyes. I can see by looking at you for thirty seconds how much love and strength you have. Look at this mom who loves you and has gotten to show you how much she supports you. So, you can't accomplish all you thought you would, but life is about more than accomplishments and job titles. Who you are is a gift to others because of what you've been through. And you need to press on because other people who are struggling need to see that you can, so they know that they can too."

A tear-filled smile spread across her face and lit up the room as I spoke to her.

What are your trials today? How are you responding? Is it with thanks?

"Triggers" are things that cause an unwilled response. Touch a hot stove and your hand automatically pulls back. Some life events can cause us to be triggered to defensiveness, anger, or fear. But you can train yourself to be triggered in particular directions.

When bad things happen—from Job-sized triggers to a mosquito bite—they usually trigger a negative response in us. But Job had trained his soul to a different kind of first response. You can too.

Every time you're annoyed, I want to challenge you to give thanks and praise to God. When I'm in traffic, I never wave with one finger. My goal is that if you cut me off, I'll raise all five fingers as I lift my hand in praise! The more we do this with small things, the more we'll be like Job when (not if) the big trials come our way.

We need to get into the habit of replacing habitual whining with habitual praising. I've heard it said that Jesus could turn water into wine, but he can't turn your whine into anything. And habitual gratitude, especially in the face of life's trials, is an urgent task. If you've ever gone for a hike, you can see where the rain runs on a trail even when it's dry. Little gullies are carved into the earth, and they get deeper with every rainfall, making their course inevitable. The way you think forms "gullies" in your mind. You can form gullies of whining or mountains of joy. It's up to you.

> "Gratitude is the first sign of a thinking, rational creature."
> —Solanus Casey

Romans 12:2 tells us to be transformed through the renewal of our minds. That's not easy, but you can do it. You can become a grateful person. It's never too late to change the patterns of thought you've established in yourself and to replace them with new patterns.

3. Say "thank you" often throughout the day.

The Jewish people have prayers of blessing and thanks for every occasion. The prayer formula begins with the words, *Baruch atah Adonai,* which means "Blessed are you, Lord," and it's often followed by "for (insert the occasion you're giving thanks for here)."

A friend of mine studied Hebrew, and once on a pilgrimage to the Holy Land he overheard an old man recite a traditional blessing that said, "Blessed are you, Lord, God of the Universe, for holes in our bodies that open and close when they're supposed to!" He laughed out loud and the old man looked at him and said with a grin, "Listen, when you're my age, that will be the most passionate prayer you say!"[3]

Everything, no matter how silly or small, is an occasion for thanks. And this is not only the case with God but with others. "Give thanks in all circumstances" (1 Thess 5:18). You need to open your mouth and say the words "thank you" many times each day.

Do it out loud right now! It only takes a second.

Doing so doesn't just give you the habit of saying "thank you" often. It creates an interior state of gratitude—a soul energized by a constant stream of thanksgiving. Like a waterwheel that generates electricity as it's moved round and round by a flowing stream, so is the soul when the mind perceives blessings and the mouth says "thank you" often.

During his 2015 visit to New York City, while at St. Patrick's Cathedral, Pope Francis said, "We have to ask ourselves, are we [even] capable of counting our blessings [anymore]?" If we don't take time to count our blessings, we forget that they're there. Thank the person behind the counter who just handed you your change. Thank a companion for his friendship. Thank your kids for letting you be their mom or dad. Thank your spouse for marrying you. Thank God for the little things every day.

Stop overlooking your daily blessings. Your friends, family, a good meal, a pretty sunset—these are the things that make us super lotto winners! Be sure to cash in with the two magic words: "thank you."

---

[3] I apologize if you find this illustration off-putting. I almost deleted but left it in because it's so wonderfully "human" and is a good reminder of the blessings of youth and middle age that I often overlook.

That's where gratitude begins. And joy is never far behind.

Rule 2:
Practice Silence

[Jesus] withdrew to the wilderness and
prayed. —Luke 5:16

IN THIS CHAPTER, we'll discuss how we've been robbed of silence by a culture of constant noise and distraction, and how that's not only robbing us of joy but making us miserable. We'll explore what recovering inner silence gives us. And, of course, how to get it.

INTRO TO SILENCE

I used to visit a monastery of hermits in Livingston Manor, New York, when I was a teenager. The hermits there each had their own hut with their own tabernacle housing Jesus in the Eucharist. Their day of work and prayer was structured so they always faced his Presence.

Even their meals, eaten alone, faced the tabernacle.

A friend of mine got to speak with one of the hermits—a rare experience—and asked if she was lonely. "Oh no!" she said. "I'm never alone!"

The hermits would gather for recreation and could talk to each other one day each week. Their meetings, I'm told, were full of joy. They'd also gather daily for communal prayer. I got to join them for the most non-rushed Mass I've ever been to. I've never seen more peaceful faces than at that monastery. They looked like they were far up Mount Sinai, covered in clouds.

They had entered a silence most of the world can only dream of. And they found God there. I learned in my few encounters with that monastery, as a teenager growing up in an increasingly noisy world, that silence isn't simply the art of shutting up. Silence isn't just an absence of noise. It's how we open up to the presence of *something more.*

Silence is the soil where joy grows, because it opens you to gratitude, creates the space for friendship to flourish, allows you to truly rest, and makes prayer possible. So, you need silence to live at least half the rules for a joyful life!

It's no wonder the devil, ever at war against your joy, has declared war on silence. Let's explore how.

THE WAR ON SILENCE: YOU SHALL BE LIKE GODS

The devil's primary weapon is temptation. And the oldest temptation in his playbook is our inherent desire to be like God, but without God's help. You may not have realized this, but you constantly get yourself and God confused. There's a difference between you and God: God never thinks he's you! That said, ever since mankind's temptation in the Garden, we've wanted to be God. "You shall be like gods" was the first temptation thrown at mankind.

Sadly, you don't play the role of God very well. When you try to be all powerful, you end up being a jerk. People have been tempted to claim that attribute of God for themselves since the dawn of time. Dictators, dominators, and manipulators have always been around.

But two new temptations to Godlikeness have become mainstream for the first time in history, and the end result of both is the near total destruction of silence in the soul.

Temptation 1: You shall be all knowing

You're tempted to be all knowing, to be connected to all information, news flows, and people, all at once. The devil no longer has to tempt you to lose yourself in the past, either out of guilt or nostalgia, or to lose yourself in the future, either out of fear or too much surety that it'll be better than the present. Nowadays, he can tempt you to lose yourself in the *mega-now*: "Take it ALL in!"

Clickbait is hard to resist, isn't it? We want to know. More and more and more and more. We want to be "on top" of everything. "You shall be like gods." It gives us the illusion of control. Godlike control.

In *Avengers: Age of Ultron*, the character Vision who

forms from computer land—a sort of incarnation of algorithms and information—is asked what his name is and, floating like a deity, he responds with the biblical name God gives himself when asked his name by Moses, "I Am." No doubt, there's an unspoken but widely held perception of deity residing in the all-knowing inter-webs. One that promises us that we too can be like gods.

Millennials, the first generation to grow up with a smartphone ever in hand, have a well-documented and sad tendency to disregard what older generations think. After all, they carry the all-knowing "smartphone" in their hand. The orb of all knowledge. The god, Vision. The oracle of information. No one can tell them anything they can't find with a quick google search. That creates a certain attitude in people.

A new business management technique has been developed in recent years for the management of millennials called "reverse mentoring." If you're an old boss and want to advise a younger employee, you have to form a relationship wherein you're asking them for advice in order to be listened to yourself. (Of course, this generalization doesn't apply to all millennials. Many are both stellar and humble human beings. I've raised a few! But this trend is very real, and a bit nauseating.)

Of course, we humans fail at *all knowing* just as miserably as we fail at *all powerful*. The more you try to take in the entirety of the present moment, the more you just end up missing YOUR moment, and the gift of YOUR present, because you've crowded it out with the "noise" of overwhelming information. There's simply no silence in a soul bombarded with *inter-webs.*

Temptation 2: You shall be all doing

The other temptation to Godlikeness that's been put into hyperdrive in recent years is our natural desire to stay on top of all tasks, all at once. God is the only Being who can really succeed at that. The rest of us actually stink at multitasking. Yet, we're constantly drawn to try it. And the dawn of the internet has drawn us into it to a degree never before experienced in history. And the "noise" of constant activity kills silence in our hearts.

> "Grief ought to be a concentration; but for the agnostic its desolation is spread through an unthinkable eternity. This is what I call being born upside down."
> —G. K. Chesterton

If you're old enough, you remember the dawn of the internet and how email became the first way of connecting online. I remember a friend telling me about email and thinking, "Why bother getting an email address? No one I know has an email, so who will I talk to? And also, why start writing digital letters when I can pick up the phone and call someone?" (And I'm only forty-four. Wow, how the world has changed in my lifetime!)

Within weeks, everyone had picked up a new @hotmail or @aol name.

I remember thinking, with each lurch forward in technology, "This is going to make us so much more efficient so we can get work out of the way and have more time for life outside of work." And then I remember watching each advance do nothing but increase work-load and work-speed expectations. And even outside of work, our personal connections have gotten so "effi-cient" that it's made our social interactions happen at an unenjoyable pace, with an expectation of immediacy that feels more like work than friendship. We might get more done and stay in touch with more people, but we're also more frantic and less happy.

We've become a world of multitaskers. We write a book while responding to texts while keeping on top of the news while updating social media while (insert your distraction here). The problem is, while everyone is expected to multitask their day away, to be *all doing*, no one is actually good at it.

The idea that you can be good at multitasking and multi-focusing is a myth. Research has shown that most people who think they're great multitaskers are actually just more distractible.[1] They're kidding themselves. We only get so much mental "bandwidth." That means that the more things you do, the less you do each thing well. The more things you're focused on, the less you're fo-cused on each thing.

Are you hyperaware of the news? Do you bear the burden of thinking you have to form an opinion about everything? Well, then you're not hyperaware of your wife's feelings. At least not at the same time and to the same degree. Is your teen present to every summons

---

[1] David M. Sanbonmatsu, David L. Strayer, Nathan Medeiros-Ward, and Jason M. Watson, "Who Multi-Tasks and Why? Multi-Tasking Ability, Perceived Multi-Tasking Ability, Impulsivity, and Sensation Seeking," *PLoS One* 8, no. 1 (2013), https://journals.plos.org/plosone/article?id=10.1371/journal.pone.0054402.

from his phone, snapchatting and eating its way into your family meal? Then he's not fully aware of the people sitting around him, even if he swears he is. Are you on top of your work email at every moment? Then you're not really on top of anything else. And each mental interruption you allow into your train of thought derails the whole train more seriously than most people realize.

There's something researchers call "attention residue."[2] It's what happens when you shift from doing one thing to another. It can take you up to twenty minutes to fully, mentally engage in your new activity, or, after that quick moment of interruption, to fully return to your previous train of thought.

So, it might seem harmless when you're writing, for instance, to let in the distraction, the "noise" of your email every twenty minutes. But that fast check might mean that you never end up *really* focusing on what you're writing. Ever. And it might seem harmless to check your email or social media every twenty minutes when you're with your family. But that means you never really focus on your family.

I'm convinced there are mathematical and literary geniuses who only reach half their potential today because they're always checking their phones. More tragically, there are families who never *really* develop their relationships with each other because mom and dad check work emails every thirty minutes, and kids check social media every thirty seconds.

---

[2] Cal Newport, *Deep Work: Rules for Focused Success in a Distracted World* (New York: Grand Central, 2016), 41–44.

THE DAMAGE OF NOISE

The Growing Problem of Noise

I'd imagine that hell is a very noisy place. The world is starting to sound more and more like it.

iGen, also called Gen Z, is the canary in the mine when it comes to constant noise, constant multitasking, and constant attention residue. And it's making them miserable. Actually, it's making them crazy.

One example, par excellence, of how the internet is owning the mental bandwidth of young people is Snapchat. It's amazing how they think it's a "teen thing" while, in fact, it's constructed by gray-haired marketing geniuses in suits. They've devised something called a "streak." Each day you snapchat with a person is one day on your streak. Friends rate their importance by the length of a streak. A thousand-day streak says something! But here's the catch: if you miss one day, your streak goes back to zero. And the public pronouncement of the importance of that friendship is . . . zero.

That means if kids might have to go a single day without their phones, they panic. Their whole digital social *existence* is at stake. If they *have to* camp with dad outside the service area, they lose all their streaks. They might as well digitally die! Teens commonly loan their phones to friends to keep their five, ten, twenty, or thirty streaks going.

In short, the Snapchat execs have found a way to pivot from serving people and keeping them connected to creating an army of teens who bear the stress of working for Snapchat so that they can increase what they charge people who want to market on their platform. It's genius. And horrendous. And it's just one of countless examples.

Add to the stress of Snapchat streaks the fact that when someone sends your teen a message on Snapchat, the sender can see that the message was received. If your teenage son makes a girl wait fifteen minutes before responding to a message, that's perceived as rude. She might as well have shown up at your dinner table and asked a question that's being ignored to her face. (Never mind that it was rude of her to crash your family dinner table without being invited.) So, that phone that should be connecting people is now disconnecting you from your teen with constant "break-in" conversations, but even more, it's become a source of anxiety in your teenager's pocket. The smartphone doesn't work for him. He works for his smartphone. Pretty dumb if you ask me. But more than dumb, our phone addiction is getting dangerous.

The Impact of Constant i-Noise on Our Happiness and Sanity

If you want to be scared, read the book *iGen* by Jean Twenge, which carefully documents the impact the internet is having on the current crop of teenagers and young adults. Among the studies cited in the book:

- One was done to investigate just how distracted young people are. They tracked the laptops of college students and found that, on average, they switched tasks every nineteen seconds. And more than 75 percent of students kept a computer window open for less than one minute at a time. They're literally tweaking out on data.

- There is a direct correlation between increased screen time during leisure and increased unhappiness.
- Suicide rates were 46 percent higher in 2015 than in 2007, the year the first iPhone was released.
- The more time people spend "connected" online, the less time they have for face-to-face relationships, and the lonelier and less happy they are as a result. (They even stay connected online when they're physically with each other. If you've been around teens, you've seen them gather together, each focused on his own phone. I suppose it's easier than awkward silence and the hard work of making friends. But it's leaving them feeling alone.)
- A Danish study of almost two thousand young people kicked them off Facebook for a week and found that 36 percent fewer were lonely, 33 percent fewer said they were depressed, and 9 percent, in just one week, said they were happier.
- Another study found that eighth graders who use social media heavily, all other factors being equal, increase their risk of depression by 27 percent.
- And in 2016, for the first time, more than half of incoming college freshmen described their own mental health as below average.[3]

---

[3] Jean M. Twenge, *iGen: Why Today's Super-Connected Kids Are Growing Up Less Rebellious, More Tolerant, Less Happy—and Completely Unprepared for Adulthood* (New York: Atria Books, 2017).

We are the most noise-bombarded generation in history, and it's literally robbing us of sanity . . . let alone joy.

I'm not saying technology is all bad, or that it's the only reason for the nosedive in our happiness. I use it regularly for my ministry. But it's like alcohol, and we need to start treating it as such. It's a mixed blessing that, if not kept in line, tends to take over and become a curse.

SILENCE IS WORTH FIGHTING FOR: HERE'S WHAT IT GIVES YOU

Again, silence is so much more than an absence of sound. Silence opens us to the presence of something beautiful. Silence is the soil where joy grows. Here's what silence gives you: six things that are so valuable and make life so much better that we need to spend a few pages thinking about them!

1. Silence and Substance

Silence is where our most meaningful work comes from. Paul's most uplifting letters were written while his adventurous soul was locked down in his own personal "quarantine" of in-house arrest for two years. Moses, David, Elijah, and John the Baptist's path to making an impact on the world led straight through the silence of the desert.

Turns out, we don't have much of worth to say until we learn how to listen. Jesus also went through the quiet of forty days and forty nights in the wilderness before launching his public ministry to blaze a path for us.

People of constant "noise" might have a lot to say but not much that will be worth remembering. None of the collective millions of hours and billions of words mankind spends typing on Twitter in 2021 will be read as a classic by the schoolkids of 3021.

2. Silence and Wonder

G. K. Chesterton said that the world is dry, not for lack of wonders, but for lack of wonder.

We take everything for granted when we get used to it. We were once in awe of the humblest things. Microwaves were a wonder. Now they take too long. Cell phones blew my mind. Now I'm angry when I drop a call while talking to a friend from Tel Aviv, halfway around the world. My first few flights blew my mind. Now I get restless if it takes more than four hours to get from Denver to New York, a journey that, not so long ago, would have taken months, and you'd have had to bury grandma on the way.

We do this with one another too. Married couples were once in awe of the gift of one another. Add years, kids, bills, and it takes hard work to not take one another for granted. We get snappy with each other over the stupidest things. We can be so close that we overlook the real presence of those closest to us and feel alone. Kids do this with their parents. I know, it's hard to fathom, but there are teens out there who ac-

> "Praise should be the permanent pulsation of the soul."
> —G. K. Chesterton

tually take their parents for granted! (Are you catching my sarcasm?)

And as we live, overlooking all our greatest blessings, we become bored, because we become boring.

Reverence, the great philosopher Dietrich von Hildebrand said, is stepping back and letting the "other" unfold before you.[4] When you crowd the other with your inner noise, with your presumptions, with your words, and when you live in a constant state of distraction, you don't actually see them at all.

Reverence is the silence that creates space between you and the world all around you—space for the world to *be*—so that you can behold it all through new eyes and once again say, "Whoa, it's a double rainbow! (or insert your everyday marvel here)."

3. Silence and Gratitude

Silence leads to reverence. Reverence leads to wonder and awe. Wonder and awe lead to gratitude. Gratitude leads to joy.

And so, true gratitude grows in the soil of silence. But it ends in quiet reverence too. Gratitude can be wordless. While it's important to "count your gratefuls" out loud, gratitude is not just about listing the items you're thankful for. On a deeper level, it's a state of mind and heart. It's a disposition that spills into every moment of the day, wherein you let reality stir your soul, and your soul delights in it—reveling in the gift,

[4] Dietrich von Hildebrand, *The Art of Living* (Steubenville, OH: Hildebrand Press, 2017). For more from von Hildebrand, visit www.hildebrandproject.org.

and ultimately, in the Giver who loves you. But that level of gratitude is only possible in the quiet heart.

We've all experienced exhilaration. There's the stoke of a roller coaster (that's more "fun" than "joy"), then there's the exhilaration of riding a wave, which gets closer to actual joy, but then there's the deep contentedness, the quiet joy of a new parent holding her baby. I call it the "new-baby bubble." It's not the stoke of the wave but the deepest depths of the ocean. The real change in that moment isn't just the addition of a new baby. It's the parent's new ability to sit and stare at the gift of life and to quiet her mind, because she's now looking at something so small but that towers over all that might distract her.

A shallow stream is loud. The Mississippi doesn't make a sound. It runs deeper. It runs in silence. So it is with the deepest gratitude.

And, if you want to enter into deeper gratitude than ever before, you need deeper silence.

4. Silence and Your Dreams

Silence is the space where dreams grow. My marriage was born in silence.

The summer after my freshman year of college, I was at a family wedding in June in West Virginia. The day after that wedding, I was filled with a desire to get to my college in Steubenville, Ohio, for Mass. It was Pentecost Sunday. I asked my dad to drive me. Would I have felt that draw if I woke up as a young man today and scrolled through social media all morning? Probably not.

I saw my friend Natalie at that Mass. Afterwards,

I went up to her and a handful of friends who were talking with her. To me, it seemed like they were all looking at her, sitting in the center. There was a light coming from her in my memory. She was amazing. "They must all see it," I thought. That's why everyone is staring at her. I gave her a hug, and it felt like family. Without much thought, I said, "love you," and she said, "love you too."

Then I forgot about the encounter and went on with my summer. Lucky for me, she didn't.

She took a long trip across the country in her car. During the hundreds of miles of silence with no XM radio, no podcasts, no phone distractions, and not even any FM radio in the deserts of Utah, all she was left with was the quiet sound of the wheels on the freeway and her thoughts.

She pondered her life and what she was looking for in a man. She pondered me. When we arrived on campus together the coming fall, she was in pursuit! It took me weeks to realize what was happening because I thought she was so far out of my league, but boy was I shocked and happy when I did!

Would her dream of our life together have grown had she enjoyed a noisy, media-filled trip across the country? Would my six children exist? Honestly, probably not.

I wonder how many people are missing their vocations today because of noise. I wonder how many dreams are never given permission to grow. And how many beautiful young women pass by good young men, but both are too buried in their phones to notice one another. I wonder how many vocations and dreams never come to fruition because they never began. As soon as silence sets in where dreams might take root, it's snatched up by noise. You've got to stay on top of your Instagram, after all!

5. Silence and Rest

Countless studies point to the fact that rest is necessary for productivity. Your brain even works through work problems when you step away from them. If you feel like you never stop working, your work quality will plummet.[5] And if you never put your phone aside, you never *really* stop working. The pings, dings, and interruptions never really cease.

6. Silence and Friendship

Silence creates space where you can really be receptive to another person. Without that receptivity, there's no real friendship. Friends who talk and never really listen aren't friends. Friends who are perpetually distracted in one another's presence aren't really friends. How could they be?

---

[5] Alex Soojung-Kim Pang, "How Resting More Can Boost Your Productivity," *Greater Good Magazine*, May 11, 2017, https://greatergood. berkeley.edu/article/item/how_resting_more_can_boost_your_productivity.

How-To

1. Stop. Breathe. Think.

There are many overlaps in Buddhist and Christian asceticism. Buddhist monks and Catholic Trappist monks do many of the same things every day. The massive way in which they don't overlap is that Christian spirituality is aimed at self-actualization. You become more fully you, more fully alive, through an immersion in the love that is God. Buddhist spirituality is aimed at enlightenment through self-negation. That's not to say they don't value love and compassion, but the end goal isn't to be fully alive—fully you—but rather, to let go of the self, which they'd call an illusion. Obviously, I'm a Christian. But that doesn't mean there's nothing to learn from Buddhist monks, for whom I have enormous respect.

Buddhists have something called "mindfulness" at the heart of their meditation. Mindfulness is about being present to the moment and occupied with the here and now. Mindfulness is the antidote to distractedness.

There's a famous Buddhist school and retreat center that has a "rain room." It's a place to simply go, sit quietly, and listen to the sound of rain.[6] As a dad with a house full of kids and pets, that sounds intoxicatingly peaceful. How beautiful, to devote a whole space to simply sitting and paying attention to something we generally overlook.

[6] Thich Nhat Hanh, *The Art of Living: Peace and Freedom in the Here and Now* (New York: HarperOne, 2017), 8.

That said, I don't have to go to a monastery in Tibet to get that. Nor do I have to build a space for it. I can choose to sit quietly and take in the simple things of life, all around me, wherever I am. Holiness and happiness are right under my nose because reality is right under my nose. All I need to take it all in is a little bit of silent stillness. A bit of mindfulness.

Where are you able to achieve that? Why not right where you are?

The ocean, for all its noise, has always helped me achieve inner silence. It helps me focus on my family better too. That's because it helps me be less distracted. It helps me dive into the moment. Over time, I learned it's not the ocean; it's my state of mind when I'm at the ocean. I'm not swimming in my own thoughts when I'm at the beach. I'm watching waves. That's my rain room. I'm "mindful." But it's not the ocean. It's the quiet within. It's me.

I don't have to go to Hawaii to get what makes me happy when I'm there. You don't have to go to your favorite place to be more present to life all around you. You just need to practice silence.

Think of yourself in your happiest place. Is it the place that makes you happy or something different in you when you're in that place? I guarantee that a huge part of what makes you happy in (insert your favorite place here) is the fact that you're not looking to go anywhere else. You've arrived! Well then, what are you waiting for? Why not sit with your eyes closed, take a deep breath, and decide "I've arrived" the next time it rains? Crack your window and give yourself three minutes to do nothing but listen to it. Or lie down on your floor, look at your ceiling fan, and rest for just a minute in quiet. Wherever you are, that's where you are.

We don't have to go into the desert for forty days and forty nights to find the quiet. Our Lord did that once but then went back to that quiet place within for many moments here and there throughout his life. I often think of St. Pope John Paul II, who led one of the busiest lives a person could possibly live. He'd often kneel in intense prayer or clutch his papal staff and cross, eyes tight shut, even during a public audience. He was grabbing a quiet moment with our Lord before he spoke to us.

Literally just sixty seconds can have a radical impact on your spirit. It also has a radical impact on your prayer. Before praying, quiet your mind, let the distractions go, take a deep breath, and be silent. Then talk to God from that space of silence you just created. Or talk to God by continuing in that silence. Don't say a lot of words. Just be. One of my favorite prayers is to stare at my San Damiano Cross and breathe in "Jesus" and breathe out "Mercy" for ten or fifteen minutes.

Stop. Breathe. Think.

When you're unpeaceful. When you need to make a hard decision. When it's time to pray. When you want to focus on the person you're with. Give yourself a minute. Sometimes that's really all it takes to make the next hour—and your life—more worthwhile.

2. Put limits on your screen time.

The average American teen spends over seven hours

of screen time per day, not including schoolwork.[7] The average adult consumes five times more information (most of it quick, passing news, not enriching and inspiring information) than their counterpart did fifty years ago.[8] And most of our screen time consists of just seconds on one thing before jumping to another. For hours each day. I'm pleading on behalf of your brain right now: *Please give me a break. I'm tired.*

Your mental focus is like a muscle. The human brain burns over three hundred calories per day. That's 20 percent of your body's energy. And the more you think, the more it burns. And like any organ, your brain can get tired. Give it a break from the bombardment of stimuli and noise.

Ironically, one of the reasons we scroll on our phones is because it's the lowest-hanging fruit for our information-seeking brains to latch on to. The problem is, when we don't stop, our brains never get a break.

You shouldn't overwork your muscles. If they don't ever get a break between workouts, you won't get stronger. Your muscle will break down. Your brain is the same way. Your ability to focus breaks down when you become accustomed to scrolling through images, glancing at pages for hours each day.

---

[7] Rachel Siegel, "Tweens, Teens and Screens: The Average Time Kids Spend Watching Online Videos Has Doubled in 4 Years," *Washington Post*, October 29, 2019, https://www.washingtonpost.com/technology/2019/10/29/survey-average-time-young-people-spend-watching-videos-mostly-youtube-has-doubled-since/.

[8] Nicole Fisher, "How Much Time Americans Spend in Front of Screens Will Terrify You," *Forbes*, January 24, 2019, https://www.forbes.com/sites/nicolefisher/2019/01/24/how-much-time-americans-spend-in-front-of-screens-will-terrify-you/#516fb7a1c67a.

The impact of screen time on our ability to think is most visible in children. One study of 4,500 kids showed that children raised with less screen time and more sleep and exercise had higher cognitive abilities. They not only knew more; they could also think more clearly. Sadly, but not surprisingly, the study had a hard time finding kids who spent less than two hours a day "plugged in" to their devices. Only 5 percent met that criterion.[9]

Take a break.

I want to challenge you to rest your mind from screens for one day each week. Make it Sunday. If that sounds too daunting, then just have everyone put their phones in a basket until sundown on Sunday. Tell the friends who are used to instant replies from you not to expect it during that time.

Sometimes, that's all it takes to break the "phone addiction" in your family. (Google "phone addiction" and you'll find a growing number of psychological studies about this reality and its impact.) And you'll be amazed at how your mind and your mood change as a result.

In addition to a longer break each Sunday, do it daily! I recently did a poll to my Twitter followers asking if time on Twitter makes them more joyful or less. 86 percent said less. And yet, there they were, on Twitter, to answer my poll! I'm not sure why we spend so much time focusing on things that make us unhappy, engaging in conversations that drag us down, or on media that makes us miserable.

---

[9] Dennis Thompson, "Can Too Much Screen Time Dumb Down Your Kid?," *HealthDay*, September 26, 2018, https://consumer.healthday.com/general-health-information-16/media-health-news-760/can-too-much-screen-time-dumb-down-your-kid-738063.html.

But I am sure that we need to get intentional about limiting our time on those things.

Commit to cutting down social media to an hour a day, and like any addict, find a friend to keep you accountable. Share your daily screen time reports with him or her.

Pick times, like dinner, when phones are put down and silenced. And put your work aside each day after a certain hour. When you stop your work each day, draw a clear line between work time and rest time. I put my phone down, spread my arms out like I crossed a finish line, and say out loud (even if no one is listening), "Work. Done." And I mean it. I don't let the noise of distraction last the entire day.

Finally, if you can't seem to get on top of your phone addiction and put it down, here's another life hack that might help: There's something called "downtime" on most phones. You can set your downtimes to where you won't be allowed to check apps you select during certain times of the day. Parent yourself! Put some limits on your own screen time.

3. Be bored.

Give yourself the space to think, "What now?" And if you don't come up with an answer, do nothing. Are you standing in line at the grocery store? Then do what we did in the nineties. Just stand there and look around. Be with your thoughts. Soak in a moment of mental quiet. You'll feed bored. You'll look countercultural. Get comfortable with that. You'll get over it, and you'll be better for it.

4. Take walks.

Psychologists have found that being in nature is the perfect rest your brain needs to kick it into a silent, mindful state. A little walk outside is just stimulating enough to keep the mind from wandering in a million directions and just relaxing enough to take the edge off your day.[10] They found that this is even true in unenjoyably cold climates! Make a quiet walk a regular part of your day, even if it's for only five or ten minutes a day.

Jesus said of John the Baptist, "What did you go out into the wilderness to behold?" (Matt 11:7). He knew the answer. When you decide to lose your constant focus on the passing things, you find everything that matters most.

JUST DO IT

All this advice is simple. So do it. I'm so sick of people not becoming as happy as they're supposed to be, as focused and present to life as they're supposed to be, as grateful as they're supposed to be, because they won't do the little things that are required to keep themselves in line. Manage your focus. Fight for silence so you can start living the life you were made for. You can do it!

[10] Newport, *Deep Work*, 187–189.

Rule 3: Love Yourself

You shall love your neighbor as yourself.
—Mark 12:31

JESUS, who taught us everything to share his joy with us (John 15:11), commanded that we love others as we love ourselves (Mark 12:31). He presumed that his followers loved themselves. That's the prerequisite for loving others, receiving love, and living the Christian life. It's the prerequisite for joy. In Rule 3, we're going to dive into exactly how to love yourself and how to conquer the joy-draining lie that you're not lovable.

LOVE AND JOY

A child who feels loved approaches life with an unshakable joy. When he's little, he's always smiling. When he's in middle school, preteen conflict doesn't turn his whole world upside down because he gets to go home to a place of stability and acceptance. When he grows into a young man who still feels that love at his back, he dives into life without too much fear of failure, because he knows, succeed or fail, he's loved anyway.

Love is the ultimate source of joy, confidence, and power. And there's no worldview that lends itself to the idea that you are loved more than Christianity. *God died for you.* Try as you will, you simply can't "one-up" that. And because of that infinite love, there's no worldview that lends itself more profoundly to joy. We'll dive into that more in Rule 9, but for Rule 3, the prerequisite for accepting that reality, and facing life with the joy and confidence it gives you, is loving yourself.

You simply can't be joyful if you don't believe you're loved. And you can't let yourself be beloved if you don't believe you're lovable. When a child starts to think he's unlovable, it doesn't matter how much love mom and dad express. It falls like rain on hard, rocky ground.

To get good at receiving love and the joy that brings, you have to (1) see yourself as lovable, and then (2) get good at loving yourself in concrete ways every day.

1. See yourself as lovable.

You're Amazing

Heresy warning: Saints (both capital S and lower case s: that is, Saints like Francis and saints like your grandma) make heaven and earth more beautiful. In one sense, that's a heresy because you can't add to the beauty and the glory of God. You can't add anything to God at all. He didn't create us because he needs us. Lovers can say to one another, "You complete me." God doesn't say that to you. He completes you, but he doesn't need you to complete him.

Yet the reason it's not a heresy is because God chose to make it this way. He chose to "need" us. God chose to let us "add" to his glory.

One way to think about how we add to the glory of God, the beauty of heaven, and the beauty of this world, is stained glass. You can't add anything to the pure, blazing white light of the sun. All the colors are already in each perfect shaft that warms the entire solar system. We're about nine-

> "Rejoice always."
> —1 Thessalonians 5:16

ty-one million miles away from the sun, and yet the smallest flowers tilt their stems to take in its rays. If we hopped onto the Starship Enterprise (yes, I'm a nerd) and blasted fifty-eight light-years away, we'd still see it glimmering in the night sky.

Yet, for all its glory and power, if you put stained glass in front of the sun's rays, it makes everything more beautiful. That's you and me. That's the saints in glory in heaven. Each one of us is hit by the light that is God—the light of Existence—and so we get to exist, but more, we get to shine that light in our own unrepeatable way.

Like a pure shaft of light hitting stained glass, or a crystal which refracts the light, each of us fills the atmosphere in a way that makes it more beautiful than it would otherwise have been without us. And I'm not just talking about what we "do" and "contribute" here on earth—as important as that is. I'm talking about who we are and what we add to the beauty and glory of heaven, simply by being there and standing near the source of Being forever.

From "Sinful Man" to "Rock"

The devil hates that thought. He's terrified of it, actually. That's why the devil works hard your whole life to get you to forget it and to make you blind to how God wants you, and only you, to glorify him forever.

The devil wants you to see yourself and label yourself in a way that directly opposes God's great plan for your soul.

This was certainly the case with St. Peter. Simon, as he was named before meeting Jesus, didn't "have it all together." That's okay, because none of us do. What's not okay is that Simon perceived his very self in this way. His identity, his dignity, and his very name were, in his mind, summed up by his flaws. In his first encounter with Jesus, Jesus was preaching to a crowd near Simon. Scripture relays how Simon was mending his nets. In other words, he had no time for the preacher and miracle worker. That was for *those* people, and he wasn't one of *those* people. He didn't choose Jesus. But Jesus chose him.

Imagine how freaked out Simon must have been when Jesus walked right up to him, interrupted his work, and got in his boat to start preaching to the crowd. Didn't he notice that Simon wasn't part of the Jesus crowd? Yet, as his divine feet stood in that fishy, smelly boat which Simon didn't have time to clean yet, something about Jesus and his powerful words captured Simon's heart.

As the crowds began to clear, Jesus turned his attention to the owner of the boat he had not been invited into. He told Simon, "Go out in the deep waters and cast your nets." "Lord," Simon shot back, "we've been at it all night, which is when the fish are caught, and haven't caught much. But if you say so, I will."

He rowed out in silence, casts his nets out, and a miracle happened. He felt a little tug. Then a bigger one. Then he started pulling the nets with all his might and, as they neared the surface, all you could see were the silver bodies of fish flapping madly. And more kept jumping in as he pulled up the nets. Eventually, they were so full that it almost sank the boat.

He looked up at Jesus. Jesus was already looking at him with a grin—his eyes, filled with hope and love, spoke volumes.

Uh-oh.

Simon could see the expectation in Jesus's eyes. He could feel the invitation coming. This was just too much! Didn't Jesus know that there's a reason Simon was tending his nets rather than listening to him preach? Take a hint! Simon couldn't take it anymore. So, before Jesus could speak a word, Simon cut him off.

He fell to his knees in that fish-filled boat and said, "Get away from me, Lord. I'm a sinful man!" He breathed a sigh of relief. He finally knows. Whew. Now maybe he'll leave me alone.

Jesus wasn't scared off. He leaned in, his smile widened. "Come and follow me. I'll make you a fisher of men." Simon had labeled himself as a "sinful man." Jesus had a new name in mind for him.[1]

Jesus took Simon and his Apostles on a long journey from Galilee to Caesarea Philippi— an ancient pagan city on the border of modern-day Israel and Lebanon. I lead a yearly pilgrimage to the Holy Land, so I've made the journey before, but in the comfort of an air-conditioned bus. It's a long trek on winding roads through very rugged, very hilly terrain. It must have been a grueling walk. But Jesus thought it was worth the long journey because it was the perfect backdrop for a very important conversation. There's a massive cliff of solid rock that looms over that ancient city, and Jesus didn't want Simon to forget that image as long as he lived.

There, before the massive slab of stone overshadowing the town, Jesus changed his name from *Simon* to *Peter*, which means "Rock."

He wanted that image seared into his mind: No little pebble, but the image of stability itself. He wanted Peter to think of that every time people said his name. "Good morning, you massive Rock!" "Rock, would you please pass the fish?" Jesus knew that self-perception determines action, and he needed Peter to act as a rock-solid leader for his Church. He needed Peter's new name to counteract the old name the devil had crafted for him, and he needed him to remember that

---

[1] Obviously, I filled in some details. The full scriptural version of the story is in Luke 5.

new name again and again and again.

Claim Your True Identity in Christ

Oftentimes our negative self-image directly counters God's calling in our lives. God needed Peter to be a rock. That's how he was to uniquely serve God on earth and glorify him forever in heaven. That's precisely why the devil worked his whole life to make Peter see himself as broken and unstable, as a "sinful man."

Of course, Peter had flaws and weaknesses that persisted throughout his life, and he had to repent and work on them, just like us. But Jesus taught him that he was more than that. That was not to be the sum of his self-perception. After he met Jesus, a "sinful man" wasn't his name anymore.

How have you mislabeled yourself? This is something we all struggle with, to one degree or another, and most people aren't even aware of it.

A woman came up to me after one of my events with tears in her eyes and said, "Chris, I've had twelve miscarriages, and for years I carried around the lie that I was cursed, and I didn't even know I was doing that to myself. Tonight, I claim the truth that I'm a beloved daughter of God!"

Two things strike me about what she said: First, that she was telling herself she was cursed. We tell ourselves things that are so horrible we'd never tell them to our worst enemies! Second, that she didn't know she was doing that.

All too often, we go through life thinking, but not thinking about what we're thinking. It's time to wake up the head game, my friends! Your *joy* is on the line. Becoming who God made you to be is at stake! If there's a war between heaven and hell, the front line is between your ears, and the central battle is over how you are seeing yourself.

Take the pen out of the devil's hand. He's a great scriptwriter. Give it back to almighty God. St. Paul tells us, "We . . . take every thought captive to obey Christ" (2 Cor 10:5). Stop listening to "the accuser of our brethren" (Rev 12:10). Combat him by renouncing the lie you believe about yourself and claiming the truth that directly opposes that lie.

Have you dealt with feeling insecure? Jesus places a crown on your head and says, "Your new name is King or Queen."

Do you feel dirty? He is at your side before a pool of the cleanest, bluest water imaginable, and he names you "Pure."

Feel powerless? "Behold the Mighty Tiger! That's you!"

Anxious and out of control? "You are the Rock!"

Sure, you have flaws, but they don't sum up who you are. You've suffered setbacks, but those are pages in your life, not the whole story. You have wounds and weaknesses, but those don't define you. You have sins, but they don't spell your name. When God looks at you, he sees something he found worth dying for. You need to see that in yourself too. But that takes spiritual vigilance and work.

Too many of God's people, whom he died for and destined for heaven, walk through life looking sick and tired because they're beating themselves up instead of aligning their self-talk with God's word. Thankfully, it's simple work to transform how you talk to yourself. But it's not easy. You have to be vigilant about your self-talk and start intentionally telling yourself the truth. If you want to live with joy, you can't afford not to.

That's step one. The other step is to back up your newfound, "positive," God-breathed self-talk with action, because, as they say, "talk is cheap" if it's never acted on. If I told my wife "I love you" every day but never acted on it, she'd catch on pretty quickly. Love that's not acted on isn't love at all. You have to love yourself in action.

2. Love yourself in action.

Think of your basic human needs. What makes you feel rested? Alive? Cared for. Like *you*? Do you give time to those things? You need to.

I shared this reflection in my book, *I AM___*,[2] and wanted to include it here:

I came home from a trip recently, and my wife was absolutely burnt out. I didn't say, "Drop, give me ten rosaries and get those dishes done." (Of course, if I had said that, those dishes may have come flying at me!) I was moved with compassion and, in one of my finer moments as a husband, I said, "Stay right there. Let me run out and get you some sushi." And it struck me: if our Lord walked into the room at that moment, he'd

---

[2] See Chris Stefanick, *I Am___: Rewrite Your Name—Reroute Your Life* (Greenwood Village, CO: Real Life Catholic, 2018).

probably have said the same thing!

We think that God is only concerned with "spiritual" things and that our basic needs like rest, cleanliness, and food, or even the little things that inspire us and make us happy, are somehow beneath him. That idea isn't from Scripture. It's not from God. We have a God who loves to take care of our basic human needs!

We have a God who washed his Apostles' feet. In one encounter they had with him after he rose, they found Jesus on the beach cooking them breakfast. There are many layers of theological meaning to that fish breakfast, but one layer was this: he wanted to cook them a nice breakfast. After he made someone rise from the dead and caused a huge commotion, he'd generally cut through the chaos with a profound phrase like this: "Get him something to eat." In other words: "The poor kid was dead. He needs a sandwich."

God takes our small and very human needs very seriously. On one level, that's because it's so hard to grow spiritually if those needs aren't met. Don't complicate things: If you can't pray well, have you been sleeping enough? If you're feeling too drained to care for someone else, have you worked out, taken a walk, read a book, or done anything that would qualify as "self-care" lately? If you're a new mom and feeling totally burnt out, have you gotten a shower in lately!?

I know, the demands of life make you feel selfish when you take a break from studying, working, or taking care of the kids to get "me time." But ironically, when you don't care for yourself, all you leave your loved ones is the most burnt-out version of yourself. There's nothing loving about that. And if you're a parent, you're teaching your children that you lack the dignity and self-worth to "waste time" on yourself, and that teaches them about their own dignity and worth.

I gave an event recently where I talked about the importance of "self-care." A young priest cried on my shoulder afterwards. He said, "*Thank you* for giving me permission to care for myself. I haven't been, and my people think I have it all together, but I'm just an empty shell. I can't inspire people if I don't take time to be inspired." He was a father with nothing left to give. He was all spent. Ever feel that way? Me too.

When you let yourself get to that place, you have nothing to give. So, if not for your own sake, love yourself for the sake of those who love you and need you! You don't have to be rich to read a good book, enjoy a meal, watch a movie, work out, take time to soak in an extra-long shower, or take a nap. You just have to claim the truth that you're worth it, and then claim the time you need to do it.

How-To

1. Speak truth to yourself.

My *I AM___* book and coaching program have helped countless people to shed their lies and begin loving themselves. I can't recommend them highly enough, not because I want to sell you something but because I want you to experience the freedom and joy of living out of the right self-perception. But for now, I want you to start here: identify the truth you most need to hear and start saying that truth to yourself in the mirror.

God didn't reveal the truth to you so you'd wait for me to preach to you. Start preaching to yourself. I can't do that for you. Neither can a boyfriend or girlfriend, spouse, or coworker. And if you look to them to make up for your deepest insecurities, you're going through life way too needy. Start preaching truth to yourself, out loud, even if it feels cheesy. And do it every morning when you look in the mirror.

2. Reject your crazy ideals.

We tried to homeschool for a time. We had all sorts of ideals about what kind of parents we'd be before we had kids. After a year of failed attempts, we realized that the "Watch a Lot of Cartoons" curriculum we were inadvertently doing wasn't working. But it took us a long time to accept that because it felt like failure. In reality, the only failure was holding on to an ideal for too long. Our kids' education suffered for it. And my wife, who kept trying to fit herself into a mold that simply wasn't *her*, suffered from her own self-imposed expectations of herself.

> "Jesus did not come to lay burdens upon us. He came to teach us what it means to be fully happy and fully human. Therefore, we discover joy when we discover truth—the truth about God our Father, the truth about Jesus our Savior, the truth about the Holy Spirit who lives in our hearts." —John Paul II

You're not cut out for everything, and that's okay! You're cut out for what God wants for your life.

And today we're not just plagued by self-imposed ideals of who we *should* be. Thanks to our media-saturated world, comparison presses in on our consciousness from every side. The average person now sees up to five thousand ads per day. The job of every ad agency is simple: to convince you that you're incomplete unless you have what they're selling. "There's something lacking in you unless you use this shampoo, drive this car, or drink this energy drink." Most of us can't name five ads we've seen today, but they have a way of slipping into your consciousness. They work. If they didn't work, Coca-Cola wouldn't have spent four billion on advertising in 2019. That's more than the GDP of some countries, and that's only one company.

Teddy Roosevelt said that "comparison is the thief of joy." Is it any wonder we're becoming so joyless? We've forgotten how to rejoice in who we are, just as we are, and with no more than what we've got.

The only action item for this is to be aware of what's going on inside your heart and to be intentional about rejecting your false ideals. They're exhausting you and robbing you of your joy.

So you're not cut out for homeschooling. Maybe God wants your kids to bless their peers in a school setting.

Or maybe you're a little quirky. Many saints were too!

Or maybe you have a few reasonably placed extra pounds around your waist. If your full-time job isn't fitness, be at peace with it and enjoy the occasional McDonald's fry without beating yourself up for it!

3. Make self-care a priority and treat yourself!

If I were the God-man (which you're lucky I'm not), my miracles on earth would have been extraordinary. I'd have turned the sky various colors. I wouldn't have healed people in ordinary ways. Forget giving sight back to the blind; I'd have given out third eyes. That would have been a hard miracle for the Pharisees to overlook!

Jesus did ordinary things. Even the resurrections from the dead he worked were for ordinary people who went on to die again a few decades later. And his very first miracle wasn't splitting a sea in two. My first miracle would have been over the top! Jesus simply turned water into wine at a wedding feast in order to keep the party going. What part of "I want you to enjoy the ordinary stuff of everyday life" are we not getting?

An African Catechism says, "God created us because he thought we'd like it." Be sure to make time to do things you enjoy: "unproductive," simply enjoyable stuff. God wants that for you. Your family and friends want you to relax and smile more too. You're more fun to be around when you let yourself have more fun.

Self-care and treating yourself isn't optional. It's as necessary for your life as gas is for your car. I'm not saying to neglect your responsibilities; I'm saying that you need to see self-care as one of them.

"But the floor is dirty, and the dishes aren't done!" you say. Newsflash: The floor will always be dirty and there will always be dishes to do. Self-care isn't something you get around to when everything else is done. It's something you need to make a top and urgent priority.

Here's an idea: Put self-care in your calendar as if it

were an important meeting. It is! It's a date with yourself. Love yourself. Don't stand yourself up. Check out for an hour a few times a week to do things that bring you to life again. What's that mean for you? A hobby? Playing your guitar? Inventing something? Reading a book? Photography? Working out? Name it. Write it down. Commit to it. Love yourself in concrete ways!

Rule 4: Have Fun

God has made laughter for me. —Genesis 21:6

THIS IS our shortest and simplest rule (in fact, it's the only rule without a separate "How-To" section because it's obvious from the content of the chapter), but don't underestimate its power.

Let's start by saying an uncomfortable truth: You used to be more fun than you are. Very few people keep the childlike gleam in their eyes. They let life make them very, very serious. They let their adult responsibilities rob them of their childlikeness.

I know a few men who have resisted this soul-killing trend. My brother-in-law is one. He served in the US Special Forces. (I could tell you more, but if I did, I'd have to kill you.) Much of his professional life between missions was spent in very, very remote places with nothing to do. Or at least, what most adults would consider "nothing to do." Andy invented board games, became a pipe maker, got into photography, and can play about five different instruments and counting. Andy can't even relate when people tell him they are bored.

My friend Fr. Peter Mussett is another. It's always a party inside his head, and even though I can't get in there, it's fun to at least be near it. Everyone loves being around Fr. Peter. He laughs. He jokes. He's taken up jeeping, metalsmithing, and kite flying and

> "The LORD takes pleasure in his people." —Psalm 149:4

is always down for a deep conversation about life and how to live it to the fullest, not because he feels like he "should" as a priest but because it's fun for him. He marvels at kites and theology in the same way—with the same perpetually "stoked" spirit.

And then there's my son Joseph. The coronavirus quarantine gave me moments of craziness where I felt like a caged animal. Joseph just saw it as free time to do a million fun things. We all envied Joey's mindset during COVID-19 lockdown!

Are you bored? Well then, when did you get so boring? Who told you that your hobbies weren't worth your time? (They don't make you money, so I guess they're not "adult" enough?) Who told you to stop being goofy? When did you train your mind to "stop wasting time"?

Do you know what happens when you give up every legitimate source of fun in your life? You drink too much. You have to have fun, after all. You just forgot how to in healthier ways. It's not that I have a problem with a sensible pour of bourbon. I don't. It's just that I have a problem with it if it's your go-to to be fun again.

And why are goofiness, hobbies, wasting time, and having fun so important? Because it keeps you rooted in a very serious reality, and it's this: the weighty aspects of life are important, but they're not *all important*.

If you're dying, it's actually a spiritually powerful thing to joke about it. Forgive me if that sounds callous, because death and dying are horrible, painful, and sad, but they don't get the final word. We win. You can remind death (and yourself) of that fact by laughing in its face as my father did after his heart attack, and as my friend Ryan's wife did before she died when she got him a plaque that says, "Till death do us part is for sissies."

If your work is overwhelming and the bills are piling up, it's a spiritually powerful thing to refuse to stress out and to play with your kids for an hour here and there. It tells them, "God is in charge of our life. Not the bills."

If you're struggling in your marriage, one of the mightiest things you can do is have fun together. If you've been married long enough, you've realized it's not all a bed of roses. That's why marriage requires a vow from which you can't back out when (not if) you want to. And in my marriage, we've faced some painful issues. I wouldn't trade those crosses for anything. They've made my beloved and me who we are together. But one of the things that's gotten us through our hard times is a commitment to fun.

We do something we call "bracketing" our problems. Bracket it. Put it aside. Deal with it later. Your problem-solving brain doesn't want to let you do that. Your brain's job is to figure everything out. Your brain tends to charge into everything. It's your job to put your brain, and your problems, in their place. Sometimes what you need is to stop, be still, forget your problems, grab some sushi, and have a laugh. Your problems will be there when you're ready to get back to them.

> "Christianity taught men that love is worth more than intelligence."
> —Jacques Maritain

Taking a break from your problems proclaims to your spouse, "You're more important than our issues." Taking a break from your work stress to be silly with your kids tells them, "You're more important than my job and our income." "Life is more than food, and the body more than clothing" (Luke 12:23), after all.

I'm not saying you shouldn't deal with your issues, but don't take yourself so seriously all the time. You'll find tremendous power to take on your issues in that mindset.

I've found that one of the best ways to diffuse a tense car ride with my family of all alpha dogs is to put silly children's songs on the radio! Works every time. It's hard to fight while listening to David Casey and Raffi because it's hard to take yourself too seriously while singing, "someone stole my socks"—and half of your fights come from taking yourself too seriously.

G. K. Chesterton said that "angels can fly because they take themselves lightly." Do you want to soar? Have fun. Be fun.

It doesn't matter what stupid joke you tell, what

"useless" book you read, or what hobby you pick up that you find fun for you. Just pick something and do it, crush it, and get stoked about little, seemingly "unimportant" stuff again.

Rule 5:
Engage Your Body in the Battle for Joy

Do you not know that your body is a temple of the Holy Spirit? —1 Corinthians 6:19

YOU MIGHT THINK you're too "spiritual" for this chapter, but you aren't pure spirit. You are a "body-soul composite." Your body has a lot to do with your pursuit of joy because it's a big part of who and what you are, and increasing feelings of happiness and well-being on a bodily and neurobiological level make the battle for a deeper, spiritual joy easier to win. So, you need to engage your body in your pursuit of the joy you were made for. Let's dive into exactly what it means to engage your body in the battle for joy and look at a few simple ways to do it.

CHANGE YOUR POSITION, CHANGE YOUR DISPOSITION

I picked up my little girl, Clementine, from school the other day. She looked like a half-deflated balloon. I said, "What's wrong, honey?" "No one wanted to play with me on the playground today," she said. With only half the air left in her voice, she continued, "I think it's because I'm . . ."

"No, no, you stop right there," I said. "There's nothing wrong with you. Don't start believing there's something wrong with you because kids didn't play with you today. You're a blessing. You're funny. You know how to love people. Anyone would be lucky to be your friend."

I could see her start to slightly reinflate.

"You know what else?" I said. "Your heavenly Father looks down on you and smiles. He set galaxies in motion and put stars in the night sky for you, he loves you so much. And your earthly dad is the world's handsomest man."

She was 70 percent reinflated by that point, so I kept inflating.

"I need to see you smile." She lit up. "Now, I need you to straighten your back and breathe in. You hold your head high. And when you walk on that playground tomorrow, I want you to do it like you're a blessing. And instead of wondering *who will play with me?* I want you to look for a little girl who's lonely and desperate for someone to play with her, and I want you to play with that little girl. I want you to be a blessing, because that's what you are."

I need to repeat that message for my Clementine to you right now. Every room you walk into, I want you to walk in like you're ready to bless people. Not like a small, timid creature, hoping no one steps on you. Walk in like a thermostat. (Yes, I know, thermostats don't walk. All analogies are limping. Bear with me.) You don't respond to the temperature of a room. That's what thermometers do. You be a thermostat. You set the temperature of the room.

> "Make me hear joy and gladness; let the bones which you have broken rejoice." —Psalm 51:8

Put your smile on, back straight, shoulders back, chest out. You're there to bless. Your heavenly Father is King of the Universe, and you're the apple of his eye. That makes you royalty: a King's favorite son or most beloved daughter. Do you believe it? If you don't, look at the cross and think about what the King of Kings did for *you*. Then start informing your brain to tell your body to carry yourself like you believe it. Then maybe you'll start to believe it.

You need to stop being the passenger of your passing thoughts and moods, letting them drive you through life. Don't call "shotgun." Get in the driver's seat. Your mood should not dictate how you carry yourself—this should be determined by how you *want* to feel, because the way you carry yourself has the power to inform you how to think and feel.

When you feel unconfident and deflated and walk around as if you feel unconfident and deflated—shoulders slumped, head bowed, like a balloon with too little air—what you're doing is reinforcing a mood you don't want to have. Your body is sending messages to your mind and heart about how to feel and what you're worth. You're practicing feeling "deflated."

How about practicing what you want to feel? Fake it till you make it. I once heard that Mother Theresa said, "If you want to love God, act like you love God." The same applies to your joy and confidence and the way you carry yourself.

One study even showed a direct correlation between posture and your chemistry. Standing confident and unafraid like a superhero, legs apart and hands on your hips, actually increases testosterone (which makes people feel powerful) and decreases cortisol (which makes people feel stressed). Another power position that does the same is sitting confidently with your hands behind your head and your feet on a table, like a BOSS. And conversely, assuming a closed position, as opposed to any more open, superhero position, has the exact opposite effect.[1]

Your position expresses your disposition, but it doesn't have to be that way. Your position can *form* your

[1] Robin S. Rosenberg, "Why You May Want to Stand Like a Superhero," *Psychology Today*, July 14, 2011, https://www.psychologytoday.com/us/blog/the-superheroes/201107/why-you-may-want-stand-superhero.

disposition. Remember, God didn't just create you as a pure spirit. You need to engage all that you are in your battle for joy!

SMILE MORE

Pope Francis, in his usual candor, criticized non-smiling Christians in a homily, "using a phrase that translates literally as 'the face of a pickled pepper'" to describe their appearance.[2] He then drove home the importance of smiling in Christian witness. People should see that we actually believe the best news in human history by simply looking at our faces.

In short: He is risen. Tell your face.

If we believe the best news in human history, it should shine on our faces. Not if we feel it—but because we believe it. And also, because smiling isn't just an expression of joy. It's a source of joy.

Proverbs says, "A glad heart makes a cheerful countenance" (Prov 15:13). The science has shown that the converse is also true. A cheerful face makes a joyful heart.

British researchers found that a smile stimulates our brain's reward mechanisms as effectively as two thousand bars of chocolate. So I guess you don't have to smile, but you might want to get eating. The same study also found that a smile stimulates the brain's re-

---

[2] Cindy Wooden, "Sourpusses Hurt the Church's Witness, Mission, Pope Says at Mass," *Today's Catholic*, May 10, 2013, https://todayscatholic.org/sourpusses-hurt-the-churchs-witness-mission-pope-says-at-mass/.

ward center as effectively, for most people, as getting a $25,000 check.[3] Want to win the lottery? Smile ten times a day and, in a month, you'll have accumulated as much sense of reward as someone who won $7.5 million.

One Berkeley study on smiling and depression found that smiling in a mirror with a really big smile for twenty minutes a day reduces depression.[4] (I'd image that twenty minutes also gives you some pretty buff cheek muscles.)

And, on the plus side, science is finding that smiling, like yawning, is literally contagious. Just thinking about it or seeing it can spread it. (Yawn. Yawn. Yaaaaaawn. Go ahead. Do it. See? I just made you yawn. Now . . . SMILE!) So, you can spread all the benefits of smiling by simply doing it yourself. How wonderful.

Mother Teresa once said, "We shall never know all the good that a simple smile can do." We're beginning to find out.

EXERCISE

Another mighty way to engage your body in the battle for joy is exercise.

There was a study done on the impact of exercise on depression. They found that, for a lot of people, work-

---

[3] Ron Gutman, "The Untapped Power of Smiling," *Forbes*, March 22, 2011, https://www.forbes.com/sites/ericsavitz/2011/03/22/the-untapped-power-of-smiling/#4c6afa0a7a67.

[4] Evan Farmer, *Breaking In: The Formula for Success in Entertainment* (Dallas, TX: ISB Publishing, 2012), 117.

ing out regularly was as effective at treating depression as antidepressant medication.[5]

Now I need to clarify: I'm not against medication if you suffer from clinical depression. In fact, I'm a big fan of it if you need that. It's not a sign of weakness that you need some help being who you are. The brain is an organ like any other, and sometimes it needs a little help balancing itself. But especially if you need medication, you need to pay attention to that study.

Depression is at an all-time high, and I think it's in no small part because of how sedentary we've become as a society. Human beings did not evolve to stare at their smartphones for ten hours a day. Our bodies were made to move. And exercise kicks off a whole concoction of happy-making neurological and hormonal processes that make our lives not only longer but also more enjoyable.

I'm not saying the exercise is enjoyable. For most of us, it's not. That's because, in addition to evolving to hunt and gather, you also evolved to conserve the calories you need to survive, so most people don't *like* a hard cardio workout. But they do tend to like the other twenty-three hours of the day more after that cardio workout. Nothing feels worse than being mid-session on a cardio workout! But nothing feels better than that finished workout!

My wife suffers from pretty intense winter depression. That's partly why we moved from Wisconsin to

---

[5] "Working Off Depression," *Harvard Health Publishing*, March 2014, https://www.health.harvard.edu/mind-and-mood/working-off-depression.

Colorado, but it's still not nearly warm enough for her. Before we realized what was going on, by the end of every winter, we'd fill our days with despairing existential conversations about life, and we'd start looking at Zillow for houses in Florida and Maui.

Last year, she started working out really aggressively four days a week. She didn't complain a single time about winter. Her seasonal affective disorder completely disappeared. And she didn't need any medication to make it go away.

Exercise is powerful. Plain and simple.

How-To

1. Go ahead. Smile.

This one isn't too complicated, but you have to be intentional about doing it.

When you greet someone, be intentional about smiling when you say hello. When you see a face at the checkout in the grocery store, every time, give a smile and say hi.

And smile at yourself too. In the mirror. Literally. That practice has serious mood-changing power.

I used to get an upset stomach before every talk I gave. For someone who speaks for a living, that's a lot of time feeling sick. I no longer do. And it's not only because I've gotten more used to public speaking. It's because I've learned how to manage my own emotions.

Before I speak publicly, I look in a mirror, breathe

in, expand my chest and arms, and smile with a smile so huge that if you walked in the room, you might think I'd lost my mind. And it's not because I feel *that* joyful. It's because I want to, and more importantly, I want to communicate joy and lift people up. And it works every time. My feelings can shift like the gears of a car from fear of talking to a large crowd to excitement.

I manage my feelings. They don't manage me. And a simple smile helps me do that. It'll help you too. But you have to make a habit out of doing that.

2. Set when and where you plan to work out.

(This helpful life hack is also in my I AM___ coaching program.)

When I say, "You should work out more," you probably think, "I know. I've been telling myself that for years. You're literally doing zero to help me right now." But maybe you need a bit more than to tell yourself, in vague terms, that you should exercise more.

In the book *Atomic Habits*, the author shares a study where British researchers conducted a test to see how they could help people improve exercise habits. People were split into three groups. A control group was simply told to record when they exercised. A second group was given a motivational talk about the benefits of exercise. And a third group was given the same motivational talk and told to write down exactly where and when they planned to exercise.

In groups one and two, less than 40 percent ended up exercising. It's worth noting that the group that was given a motivational talk may have felt motivated in the moment, but it made no difference in their behavior compared with the group that was simply told to write down when they'd worked out. But for the group that heard the motivational talk *and* went through the mental work of writing down where and when they planned to exercise, 91 percent developed better exercise habits that lasted![6]

You need to exercise. You know that. But if you want to do what you know you need to do, you need to write down when and where. And you need to stop dialoguing with yourself about why you don't want to work out. That's irrelevant. Remember: not all of your thoughts and feelings get a vote!

> "We are half-hearted creatures, fooling about with drink and sex and ambition when infinite joy is offered us, like an ignorant child who wants to go on making mud pies in a slum because he cannot imagine what is meant by the offer of a holiday at the sea. We are far too easily pleased."
> —C. S. Lewis

And don't complicate exercise. There are great online programs and personal trainers, and I'm a fan of all that. But you can also keep it very, very simple. If you have no idea what to do, but you wrote down "work out" on Monday at 8 a.m. in your planner, put some gym shorts on at 8 a.m. and do jumping jacks until you want to pass out. It'll probably only take you about five minutes! Then two days later at 8 a.m., you'll do three more minutes of jumping jacks.

---

[6] James Clear, *Atomic Habits: An Easy & Proven Way to Build Good Habits & Break Bad Ones* (New York: Avery, 2018), 69–70.

I guarantee it. You'll get stronger. It's how the body works. But more importantly, you'll get happier.

I love workout variety: lifting weights, doing HIIT workouts, boxing, jujutsu, you name it, but when I'm on the road, I just do burpee push-ups. Look it up. It's grueling. If that's all I did for as long as I could three days a week, I'd probably be in great shape. There's no need to complicate exercise unless it's fun for you to do so.

A quick (but important) tangent about exercise: Be sure to kill crazy ideals.

I know a professional bodybuilder. "There's no way we should call this a fitness sport. There's nothing healthy about it," he told me.

Before a competition, he has to cut his calorie intake to five hundred calories a day. That's while keeping up his hours-long weight-lifting regimen. Then, a few days before a competition, he drinks no water at all so that his skin, devoid of any hydration, sucks itself to his muscles. "Before I go onstage to pose," he said, "I can't think straight or speak in complete sentences."

And it's in this state that people have their pictures taken and put on the front of a workout DVD, appear in movies shirtless, take the stage at a competition, or pose for a billboard, sending the message to the world that *you too can look like this.*

No, you can't, actually. Unless it's your job.

Hugh Jackman, who played Wolverine in *X-Men*, was shirtless in one scene, and I was amazed that a guy in his forties could look that fit. I did some research into what his workout and eating routine were, only to find that he had so dehydrated himself for that scene that he needed an IV immediately after filming it. Yet countless men saw that movie and set that image as their fitness goal.

If your workout is driven by vanity and an unrealistic body goal, or if your sense of accomplishment is too tied to it, it won't make you happier. It'll rob you of peace. Your workout time will be bogged down with undo stress. Your whole day will revolve around it. And you might push yourself so hard you get injured. You've heard the saying "no pain, no gain." I have another one for you: "no pain, no pain."

If you want your workouts to make you more energetic and joyful, be sure to remind yourself of that motive before you hit the gym.

3. Make your body an offering.

Someday, your body will no longer work. Sadly, this one's not an "if" but a "when." We refer to people whose bodies don't work as they were designed to as "disabled." But, in a very real sense, the rest of us are just "temporarily abled." We can do things to push off our inevitable demise, but that doesn't change the inevitability of it. That's not pessimistic. It's reality. And because we're body-soul composites, that's not easy.

So, how do you engage your body in the battle for joy when it's not working right? St. Paul tells us in Romans 12:1, "Present your bodies as a living sacrifice, holy and acceptable to God, which is your spiritual worship."

If you're an old-time Catholic, you've heard the

phrase "offer it up" in response to suffering. That sounds insensitive, but there's real wisdom in it. Jesus suffered on the cross, not so we wouldn't have to but so we'd know how to. For us Catholics, suffering isn't something we try to forget or overlook. It's a part of life that we have to embrace, and we can do that by uniting it to Jesus's offering on the cross for the salvation of the world.

Paul wrote of his own physical suffering in Colossians 1:24: "I rejoice in my sufferings for your sake, and in my flesh I complete what is lacking in Christ's afflictions for the sake of his body, that is, the Church." Of course, nothing is technically "lacking" in what Jesus did on the cross, but Jesus chose to make us "co-redeemers" with him, so to speak, able to spiritually extend the fruits of the cross to the whole world by our prayer and sacrificial offering when we suffer. I think God set things up that way to give purpose and joy to our pain. As Paul said at the beginning of his statement to the Colossians, "I rejoice in my sufferings." A love-infused sense of purpose leads to joy, even in our suffering.

4. Sleep.

God doesn't often bypass the laws of nature any more than he would go around the laws of grace. He made both. Both come from him at every nanosecond. Sometimes, when you feel a general angst about life, instead of panicking about your state and relooking at everything you might need to change, you just need a good nap!

It really is amazing how many problems we could avoid if we just slept like we need to. Teens, for instance, need eight to ten hours of sleep every night. Only 15 percent of them get that much sleep. Lack of sleep can make you forgetful, give you more pimples, make you aggressive and impatient, and can lead to sugar addiction, a dependence on too much caffeine and nicotine, and unsafe driving.[7]

It seems like half the problems we see in the "typical teenager" that cost society billions in mental health care, behavior problems at school and home, teen driving accidents, and dermatological problems could be solved if teens stopped stimulating their brains by scrolling on their phones at bedtime, shut the lights off, and slept like they needed to. We tend to look for such expensive and complicated solutions to such simple problems.

And this obviously doesn't just apply to teens, but everyone. If you want to be healthy and happy, you can't sacrifice your sleep. In addition to making you generally less "fussy" and better able to fight for your daily joy, sleep helps you break down sugar (i.e., shaves off fat), strengthens skin, bone, and muscle, shrinks brain cells to "squeeze out" debris, and fights off everything from Alzheimer's to depression.[8] Sleep is more powerful for your body, mind, and mood than any drug. I'll never forget a homily I heard in college. Fr. Brian Cavanaugh,

---

[7] "Health Tip: Most Teens Don't Get Enough Sleep," *HealthDay*, January 31, 2012, https://consumer.healthday.com/kids-health-in-formation-23/misc-kid-s-health-news-435/health-tip-most-teens-don-t-get-enough-sleep-660912.html.

[8] Alice Park, "The Power of Sleep," *Time*, September 11, 2014, https://time.com/3326565/the-power-of-sleep/.

TOR, said, "Sleep is a weapon." If you want to fight for your joy, be sure to use it.

Rule 6:
Make Friends

You are my friends. —John 15:14

IN CHAPTER 1, I mentioned Harvard's unprecedented study of 268 people over the course of 75 years to find out what would make people thrive in old age. More than good genes and lots of money, it was joy!

So, how to get it? The Harvard study also explored that. Turns out it's not money, fame, success, or even health. It's friendship. People with good, healthy relationships ended up being happy and healthy into old age.[1] But that's not easy, which is why this rule isn't "enjoy friends" but the verb our parents used when they commanded us to get out and play: *make* friends.

---

[1] Mineo, "Good Genes Are Nice, But Joy Is Better," *The Harvard Gazette*.

FRIENDSHIP: IT'S GOOD FOR YOU

More and more studies are showing that loneliness is literally toxic. "The increased mortality associated with loneliness is equal to the increased mortality we see with smoking 15 cigarettes a day . . . [and is] greater than the mortality associated with obesity."[2] That's right, smoking and eating bacon every day with friends is healthier than being lonely! (Not that I recommend either!) Conversely, living in community extends your life.

> "No soul that seriously and constantly desires joy will ever miss it. Those who seek find. To those who knock it is opened."
>
> —C. S. Lewis

In Haiti, the mission that we work at with Real Life Catholic started an orphanage. While working with orphans, they found old people dying alone in the hills and the forest. So, they started a home for the dying to give people a comfortable bed to die on. And a miracle happened. The kids from the orphanage started coming over and playing with the elderly in the home for the dying . . . and they stopped dying. What was a hospice became an old-age home where people live to a ripe old age!

One study of over seventy-five thousand women done over sixteen years shows that those who attended church more than once a week had a 33 percent lower risk of death from any cause over those who didn't attend, and those who went just once per week had a 26

---

[2] "Feeling Lonely, You're Not Alone," *CBS News*, February 10, 2019, https://www.cbsnews.com/news/feeling-lonely-you-are-not-alone/.

percent lower risk of mortality. Kind of gives "I came so they might have life" a new, literal level of meaning![3] Another study found that people who go to church regularly live almost four years longer than people who don't.[4] No doubt, that's because of how faith gives people energy and hope, but it's also because church is a place where community happens.

And, of course, it's not hard to see how friendship is also spiritually healthy.

FRIENDSHIP: A SPIRITUAL PILLAR

A great analogy for the spiritual power of friendship can be found in the world's largest trees. Sequoias are the biggest trees on earth. Among their most famous is the General Sherman Tree. Its base circumference is over 100 feet, and it stretches almost 275 feet into the air. Its estimated weight is 6,167 tons. The fire-resistant bark of a sequoia can be up to two feet thick. Some sequoias on earth today are over three thousand years old and are still healthy and growing. Hiking in a sequoia forest is one of the strangest experiences I've ever had. I felt like an ant. It's was so eerily beautiful—and also dangerous. On a windy day, they call sequoias "quiet killers." Something as harmless as a branch falling

---

[3] Nicholas Bakalar, "Churchgoers May Live Longer," *New York Times*, June 12, 2016, https://well.blogs.nytimes.com/2016/06/12/churchgoers-may-live-longer/.

[4] Rachael Rettner, "Could God Help You Live Longer?," *Live Science*, June 13, 2018, https://www.livescience.com/62809-religion-longevity.html.

silently to the ground is, for a hiker, the equivalent of having a regular-sized tree suddenly fall on you.

But the most shocking thing about the mighty sequoia is this: their roots only go about five feet deep. How, you'd ask, can such a mighty tree stand with such shallow roots? It's simple: their roots don't stretch deep. They stretch wide. They interlock with a forest of other mighty trees. Just so, the only way to grow into our full stature as children of God is to be connected with other Christians at our roots.

Jesus didn't just talk about this. He modeled it. He loved everyone, preached to the multitude, invested his life in the twelve, and leaned on the three: Peter, James, and John.

Few things could be as important for our health and happiness as friendship. But it's not easy. Let's dive into how to push through the struggles and form real-life friendships.

How-To

The soil where friendship grows is time, intimacy, and mercy.

1. Put in hard time.

Friendship takes time and effort. That's why this rule might be the easiest to grasp but the hardest to live.

The human mind is hardwired to choose comfort with the least effort possible and to avoid pain. Friends don't fit that paradigm. They can take a lot of effort.

You know what does fit that low-effort, low-risk paradigm? Online "friends."

That's why our cavemen brains tend to favor them. Think about it. When you feel the discomfort of loneness, do you (a) call a friend and have coffee together, or (b) scroll on your phone until you've drowned the loneliness for a moment? More and more people are picking option b, and it doesn't work. Digital connections are real, but they are not deep enough. Virtually every study on iGen shows that the more phone interaction replaces face-to-face interaction, the lonelier people become.[5]

The truth is that making real friendships takes way more time than a fast text, snap, or retweet.

Making friends requires setting aside distractions to converse or share an interest. The problem is you're busy—but you have to make time for what matters! For your emotional, physical, and spiritual health, you have to make time for friendships to grow.

Set aside time in your calendar every week to connect with one of your friends, or the same friend, for coffee, a phone call, or some other shared activity.

2. Be intimate.

Real friendship is intimate. Most people today associate intimacy only with romantic relationships. They're doing it wrong. That misperception is probably why

5   Rowena Gonden, "Social Media Linked to Increase in Depression among Teens, Young Adults," *Healthline*, March 20, 2019, https:// www.healthline.com/health-news/social-media-linked-to-mental-health-disorders-in-igen-generation.

so many men end up lonely—63 percent, to be exact.[6] They fear that a deeply loving relationship would imply romance. It might also be why so many teens end up enmeshed in physical relationships with friends. The human heart needs intimacy. And if no one asked teen X to the dance, she might turn to her friends to get the intimacy she needs, but in the wrong way.

Friendships should be intimate! That's how Jesus did friendship. Jesus didn't tell the Apostles, "You guys are my work buddies." He said, "You are my friends" (John 15:14). To his friends he said, "I have earnestly desired to eat this Passover with you . . . this is my body" (Luke 22:15, 19). He didn't say, "Man has no greater love than this, to snuggle with his girlfriend on Valentine's Day." He said, "Greater love has no man than this, that a man lay down his life for his friends" (John 15:13). To his friend, Peter, he said, "Do you love me?" to which Peter replied, "Yes, Lord; you know that I love you" (John 21:15). Now there's an awkward conversation between two dudes. But they were no less manly for it. Can you tell your friends that you love them? I do all the time.

> "Encourage one another and build one another up, just as you are doing."
> —1 Thessalonians 5:11

I want to give you a secret formula for forming

[6] Elena Renken, "Most Americans Are Lonely, and Our Workplace Culture May Not Be Helping," *National Public Radio*, January 23, 2020, https://www.npr.org/sections/health-shots/2020/01/23/798676465/most-americans-are-lonely-and-our-workplace-culture-may-not-be-helping.

deeper friendship. As a spiritual discipline, I want you to get together with one to five friends once a month. Grab a cup of coffee. Pray. Do a small group Bible study if you want to. But be sure the conversation lands on this secret formula for creating friendship. Get out your pen and write this magical phrase down. Ready? Here it is: *How are you?*

I don't just mean "How do you feel today" but "How are you *really* doing?" Another way to ask this is "What is God doing in your life?" Or maybe the 1, 2, 3 of: "What are you grateful for? What are you struggling with? And how do you want to grow?" The bottom line is to check in, deeply, so that you can know and be known, and like sequoias, you can hold each other up.

And then, after really listening to one another, pray for each person based on what they said, and get together and repeat that every month. It's so simple. So directed. And it can change your life, making you happier, healthier, and holier.

Scripture says, "Iron sharpens iron, and one man sharpens another" (Prov 27:17). Conversely, without any gut-level checking in and honest accountability, you might as well be a sequoia without any roots. Frankly, I don't care how big and strong you look, a little storm is bound to blow you over.

Find friends to do this with by reaching out and asking them. Tell them, "I know we're friends, but I'd love to go deeper. I'd love to get together once per month and just spiritually check in so we can pray for each other and grow together." If they happen to be reading this book too, just ask them, "Will you be my special friend?" They'll know what you mean!

None of this is rocket science. Like every simple and powerful rule in this book, you just need to make time for it.

3. Be merciful, and let things go easily.

People are annoying. Stick around me long enough and I'm bound to annoy you. But the reality is that, according to the Harvard study we referenced, even difficult relationships are good for you! The positive health impact of friendship still applied to old married couples who bicker a lot. The key wasn't "smooth" relationships but a sense that they loved one another, were faithful, and could rely on each other. Old people with those kinds of relationships in their lives, romantic or not, still felt the aches and pains anyone else does in old age, but they didn't feel them as strongly.

So, how do you have long-term, supportive relationships with people who are bound to annoy you? In the words of Elsa, "Let it go."

You tend to find and focus on the flaws of the people in your life, don't you? That's because your brain is hardwired for self-preservation and survival. We're good at finding and avoiding things that might hurt us.

I'm not saying to be blind to the flaws in other people, but to choose to let it go more often. The only way to grow in friendship over time is to forgive easily. Refuse to let unforgiveness destroy your friendships and your joy. Francis of Paola said, "Unforgiveness is like a worm in your mind."

It's helpful to remember that half the time when

people offend you, they didn't even know what they were doing. And guess what, half the time you offend people, you never even know it happened. Mistakes happen all the time.

My uncle was in New York City recently walking down the street. Pickpockets there are very good at bumping into you and taking your wallet out of your pocket without you even knowing it. It's an art. He bumped into a guy who was jogging by and reached into his pocket to find his wallet was missing. He ran up to the guy and said with a stern voice, "Give me the wallet." The jogger stopped dead in his tracks, took the wallet out, and handed it to my uncle.

My uncle called home and said, "Marge, you'll never guess what just happened to me." She said, "Paul, your wallet is on the kitchen table!" Of course, he sent the wallet he had accidentally stolen back with an apology note and no return address.

Mistakes happen. People hurt each other. You hurt people. You don't have to dive in and figure out that person's motives. You don't have to get on somebody else's crazy train. Just let things go more easily, for your own sake.

Forgive as God has forgiven you. Not because people deserve to be forgiven but because you deserve the freedom of forgiving and the joy of friendship. In the Lord's Prayer, we say, "Forgive us our debts, as we also have forgiven our debtors" (Matt 6:12, NIV). When someone wrongs you, they are indebted to you. By justice, they owe you. Let it go. You have a right to hold on to your anger for the rest of your life, but you only have about thirty thousand days to live. Don't waste any on holding grudges that can destroy relationships in your life.

You might deserve to hold that sin over your husband's head for the rest of his life. You might deserve that your kids treat you better than they do. And you are entitled to friends who don't rub you the wrong way. But above all, you're entitled to happiness. People aren't easy. Get over it so that you can experience the blessing it is to have long-term, meaningful, supportive friendships with other people who are as imperfect as you are.

Rule 7: Rest

Rest a while. —Mark 6:31

YOU CAN'T HAVE JOY without resting from your work. Frankly, you can't even remember who you are without rest. The command to rest and worship on the Sabbath changed the world. Obeying that command will change your life. In this rule, we'll simply focus on the *rest* part of Sabbath. Like worship, rest isn't something that's handed to you. You need to fight for it.

THE LAMPLIGHTER

We can all fall into a kind of slavery to our work if we're not careful. We can all lose ourselves under the crushing wheels of our schedules and "to-dos" if we don't keep them in check.

In the book *The Little Prince*, a space-traveling young prince visited a small, lonely planet occupied by one small man, with one seemingly small job. He was a lamplighter. His job was easy enough until, over the years, his planet sped up, rotating 1,440 times every twenty-four hours. That's 1,440 days and 1,440 nights for every earth day. So, faithful to his commitments and never asking why, the lamplighter interrupted his conversation with the little prince every sixty seconds to dutifully light his lamp at sundown and extinguish it at sunrise.

The lamplighter was a man who made a living that ended up taking over his life. Work had served a purpose, and then as work sped up, he knew not how, every aspect of his life ended up serving his work.

Have you ever felt that way about the "gears" of your life? Work. Kids' sports. The laundry. It all serves a purpose, and then at some point, the scales tip, we know not how, and it takes over.

It robs you of more than your time. If you're not careful, it robs you of your sense of self. It feels like slavery.

Don't panic.

The people of God have been there before, and the way out of slavery is fairly simple. It's Sabbath.

THE SLAVES AND THE SABBATH REVOLUTION

Life wasn't fun as a Hebrew slave 3,300 years ago in Egypt. The work never stopped. Ever. "Slave" wasn't just a job title. "Slave" is what they *were*. That is, until God stepped in.

The Maker of all only had Ten Commandments for

mankind. For all the accusations of God being an over-bearing "boss," that's a pretty short list. And one of the ten is this: I want you to relax from your work—making time for rest and for worship—one day every week. (Or in biblical language, "Keep holy the Sabbath.") Sounds easy enough. But think for a minute about how radically countercultural a command to rest was in the ancient world. It actually started a war.

The entire rift between the Hebrew slaves and their Pharaoh was about resting from work. God had commanded his people to a "holy party"! The famous words of Moses to Pharaoh, to "let my people go," was so that they could obey a command from God to "hold a feast to me in the wilderness" (Exod 5:1).

That command to hold a festival, and ultimately the Commandment to keep the Sabbath, was about far more than a request of the Jews to have a work break so they could crack open a beer with friends, and Pharaoh knew it. It was a declaration of war on an entire lifestyle. It attacked the very fabric of their slave society. On the surface, it was about rest and worship, but on a deeper level, it was about freedom. It was about putting work, and Pharaoh himself, in his place. The Sabbath has forever put kings and bosses in their place, saying to them, "There's an agenda for mankind that is higher than yours."

The Hebrews no longer existed to serve earthy kings. Their name was not to be reduced to functionality, "slave," but raised to relationship, "God's chosen people."

The concept of a Sabbath was revolutionary, and it

still is when we actually live it.

How Sabbath Changed Society

We weren't born to live as cogs in a great societal machine. We don't exist for (insert your Pharaoh here). We are not a "means to some other end." Of all creation, we are "the only creature on earth which God willed for itself."[1] God made us to share in his joy, simply because he loves us. We aren't human doings. We are human be-ings. The thought of *you* (not what you can *do*) delighted God. That's why you exist!

> "This is the day which the LORD has made; let us rejoice and be glad in it."
> —Psalm 118:24

Perhaps a simpler way to say it is this: humans aren't "tools." If the Church doesn't budge on issues like abortion, pornography, euthanasia, the dignity of immigrants, and the rights of workers, it's not because of how we think about politics. It's because of how we think about human beings.

Human beings don't exist for convenience, the factory, government, commerce, or the sciences. Our lives aren't to be sacrificed on the "altars" of any of those things. All those things exist to serve us. When we forget our high place in creation, we become cogs in so many machines. When we forget our dignity, work has no limits, individual rights no longer matter in rela-

---

[1] Second Vatican Council, *Gaudium et Spes* (1973), §24. (This was John Paul II's favorite Vatican II document, which he had a role in writing as a young cardinal.)

tion to government, people become sexual commodities for sale, and the sciences have no boundaries when it comes to bioengineering, genetic manipulation, or human trials.

We matter. We have dignity and rights. That idea didn't come from nowhere. The idea of our high place above the ever-turning wheels of civilization is the bedrock of Judeo-Christian culture, which, despite the decline in church attendance, we still enjoy today—thanks to the Lord of the Sabbath who put Pharaoh in his place.

How the Sabbath Changes You

Keeping the Sabbath has the power to keep you grounded in who you are and in the present moment.

Back to Yourself

The Sabbath isn't just about a cultural or societal revolution. The Sabbath calls us to a personal revolution: to revolt against the idea that our value comes from what we do, or that our identity is no more than our job title.

It's so easy to forget ourselves, our hobbies, our fun, the things we enjoy about ourselves and that others like about us. We need to give ourselves space to rest so we can simply rediscover ourselves again. Every week, we're summoned to remember who we are. We are more than the things we do or the roles we play. This even applies to our most noble roles in life.

A minister met my mother once, and she introduced

herself as "Christopher's mom." He had to ask about three times who she was before she realized what he was doing. When she finally said her name, he chided, "Yes, you're Mary. You're not just Christopher's mom." Even motherhood can't sum up all that a person is.

We objectify ourselves when we don't remember that. When we never rest from our working, giving, and serving, we lose our sense of self. Our identity melts in the great cauldron of work. In the words of the old Rush song:

> Yes, I'm workin' all the time.
> It seems to me
> I could live my life
> a lot better than I think I am.
> I guess that's why they call me,
> they call me the workin' man.
> I guess that's what I am.[2]

You are more than the things you do. Being disciplined about your weekly rest can help you remember that. So revolutionary! So simple!

Back to the Present

In addition to helping us recover our sense of self, the Sabbath is our weekly practice at embracing the present moment—which is the only time that overlaps with eternity. That's right, embracing *now* helps us embrace a bit of heaven on earth.

The Sabbath—that day of rest given to the Jews—

---

[2] Rush, "Working Man," recorded 1973, track 8 on *Rush*, Moon Records.

had always been on Saturday. Christians transferred their Sabbath to Sunday because it's the day Jesus rose, but also, symbolically, because it's the eighth day of the week. Of course, you're thinking, "There's no basement at the Alamo, and there is no eighth day!" Precisely! There's not. To enter the eighth day meant to break the cycle of time and enter eternity. On the eighth day, outside the wheel of time, there is only one moment, and it's the moment we tend to overlook the most: Now. (Ironically, *now* is the only time we've ever really had.)

> "Take my yoke upon you, and learn from me; for I am gentle and lowly in heart, and you will find rest for your souls."
> —Matthew 11:29

How is the present most like eternity? You've experienced it. Have you ever lost track of time with a beloved? Or while looking at waves? Or at a great meal? The longer we bore into a present moment, the closer we get to piercing through the veil of time altogether. "Where has the time gone?" we wonder.

A similar experience can be had sitting with a loved one who is nearing eternity in an ICU. It isn't enjoyable like wave watching, but it's no less real. Eternity is opening its gates, and we get some of the blast of eternal air from the other side. There's a dizzying loss of the sense of time. A strange sweetness piercing the pain.

The Sabbath is about learning to rest in *the eternal now*. That's where God, and every gift of your life, is waiting for you. That's why the devil is always at work to separate you from it.

He'd like you to dwell in the "mega-now" that we discussed in Rule 2. Or excessively in the future, or in the past. Anything but the present moment given to you. C. S. Lewis's must-read book, *The Screwtape Letters*, is about an old demon, Screwtape, advising his young demon nephew about how to snatch a soul from the "Enemy" (Screwtape's name for God) and lead him to hell. In one dialogue, he impresses upon his young pupil the importance of keeping the soul away from the present moment at all costs:

> The humans live in time but our Enemy destines them to eternity. He therefore, I believe, wants them to attend chiefly to two things, to eternity itself, and to that point of time which they call the Present. For the Present is the point at which time touches eternity. . . .
>
> Our business is to get them away from . . . the Present. . . . We want a whole race perpetually in pursuit of the rainbow's end [the future], never honest, nor kind, nor happy now, but always using as mere fuel wherewith to heap the altar of the future every real gift which is offered them in the Present.[3]

Ouch. To turn every present gift into "fuel wherewith to heap the altar of the future." How many times have I done that, ever working for what lies around the bend? John Lennon said that "life is what happens to you while you're busy making other plans."

[3] C. S. Lewis, *The Screwtape Letters* (New York: HarperOne, 2001), 75–76.

You work so hard to "grow up," and then you work for your job, then your marriage; then while you're married, you work for a kid; then when your kids come along, you're working for a more stable life; and once you've got that, you work for your retirement. The forward motion never stops. We're called the human "race" for good reason.

Then, in retirement, you remember the good old days. But what if you're in the good old days now?

I'm not saying you shouldn't make plans, but when will you finally say, "I've arrived! I'm here! Sure, I still have to work hard, but it's time to start enjoying life!"? How about today? How about right now? How about you start by being really intentional about doing that one day every week: your Sabbath?

HOW-TO

The Jews of old took the Sabbath very, very seriously. To break it meant death. To this day, you can see the highest point of the temple in Jerusalem, where the devil took Jesus to tempt him (see Luke 4). It's where the trumpeter stood to announce the Sabbath. And there, hewn into the rock where he stood, was a place to immediately drop his trumpet as the day of rest began, because if he carried it for a moment after the Sabbath began, he'd have been put to death for working.

While capital punishment for breaking the Sabbath ended long, long ago (thank God), ultra-Orthodox Jews to this day observe it with an intensity that seems to be more burden than rest. They have something called

"Sabbath elevators" in Israel. They consider the pushing of an elevator button "work." So, they have to stand in the Sabbath elevator as it waits for a long time to pick up passengers on each floor. It might take fifteen minutes to get back to your room from a hotel lobby in a Sabbath elevator.

My first time in the Holy Land, I wasn't aware of this phenomenon and offered to help one family that had been standing for about five minutes in a beeping elevator. The father snapped at me that it was a Sabbath elevator. I'm sure he was thinking, "I know how to push a button, pilgrim!" (I'd have been thinking the same thing.)

I was taken aback by his response and was grateful that we Christians no longer have to observe the letter of the law as our older brethren in faith, the ultra-Orthodox Jews, still do. But then I thought more deeply . . . there's something about the letter of the law that makes it easy to preserve the heart of the law. If ultra-Orthodox Jews go too far in observing these laws, we go too far in forgetting them.

So, here are a few non-burdensome to-dos to help you preserve the spirit of the Sabbath in your life. As always, the "how-tos" for this rule are very simple. But if you stick to them, they will transform your life.

1. Wage war on work, one day, every week.

Winnie the Pooh said, "People say nothing is impossible, but I do nothing every day!"

"Doing nothing," it turns out, is pretty dang difficult. That's why we tend to fill every waking moment with "something." If you're sitting still, check that phone. If it's a sunny day, cut that lawn. If you're enjoying your life, feel a little guilty that you're not doing the dishes. It's as if there's a little invisible Pharaoh at our backs whipping us and pushing us onward.

The coronavirus taught me how to slow down better than ever. Quarantine unleashed some powerful blessings in my life. It also absolutely stunk. Make no mistake, I'd have preferred that it never happened. But every trial has a blessing hidden in it, and COVID-19 was no exception. It was probably the only time in my life, and in the lives of millions, when the train of perpetual forward motion was derailed and I got to reexamine everything. Most people only get to do that on their deathbeds.

It brought out one of the best confessions in my life.

I found myself not traveling for the first time in ten years. I relooked at the ways my weekly travel schedule has impacted my family. I wouldn't trade my work for anything, but if my eyes were more wide open to the toll a parent's regular travel has on kids, I'd have done some things very differently.

I have a very exciting job. I love my kids more than my work (more than almost anything, actually), but in my exuberance for my work, I don't think they've always known that. "Surely that trip to film in Alaska must be more exciting than playing *chutes and ladders* with me," they thought. Stepping back from my travel enabled me to see how some of those lies had rooted themselves in my children's consciousness and how I could have done better at weeding them out.

During the coronavirus, I found myself "doing nothing" more often—playing more with my children. Taking more walks. Praying more family rosaries. I was still very busy, but in a different way, and I found myself making time for the stupidly simple little things I should have been doing all along. But it's easy to forget those things when your little planet has sped up to 1,440 sunsets a day.

I confessed this to my priest. I apologized to my children. It was incredibly healing for me to hear, "I forgive you, Dad. And I couldn't have asked for a better dad." Kids can be very merciful.

To quote Pooh again, "Doing nothing often leads to the very best of something." On Sunday, do nothing. The very best of something will fill the space. Sunday isn't the day to catch up on "work work," and it's not the day to catch up on housework. Sunday is the day to do no work.

If it didn't get done in the other six days that week, don't worry, it'll be waiting for you on Monday. There will always, always, always be work to do. You have to choose to not do it sometimes, or it'll rob you of all that matters most in life. You don't work so that, once it's done, you can get to your rest. You have to decide, at some point, to simply rest even if the work isn't done, because rest, family time, prayer, and self-care are more important than the things you "have to" do.

And this is not just a suggestion from Chris so that you can preserve your family and enjoy what matters most in life. This is a Commandment from God.

And, in addition to the command to rest and worship on Sundays, I'd encourage you to have a firm cutoff time for work every day of the week. Segment your life better. When it's time to work, work. When it's time to stop and enjoy your family, stop working and enjoy your family. Reject the gnawing sense while doing the one that you should be doing the other. You can't serve two masters at one time. There is a time and a place for everything (see Eccl 3.)

The Jews have a simple ritual of lighting a candle as the sun sets Friday night to mark that the time of rest and worship has begun. I recommend doing the same as the sun sets Saturday night. I also recommend having a little ritual every day to delineate work from rest. Each day when I'm done working, I close my laptop and say out loud, "Work! Done!" It's very simple, but it really helps me to mentally transition from work to rest.

2. Savor moments.

Rest isn't about finding shallow distractions from reality. It's about grabbing hold of life and living it more deeply. What's that look like? As is the case with most profound realities, it's actually pretty simple. I'll give you just a few ideas:

Stop and Smell the Roses

I went on a trip with my family recently to a warm place, and I kept losing my then eighteen-year-old son. He's currently a combat medic in the US Army. I'm very proud of him. But every time I lost him, he wasn't buried in his phone. He was buried in a flower. He's like

Ferdinand the Bull.

"Ethan, where were you?"

"Dad, you *have* to come and smell this gardenia," was the reply.

God gave us the smell of flowers so we'd take a moment to smell them. Ever hear the saying, "Stop and smell the roses"? Why do we take that figuratively? I can almost hear God in heaven looking down and shouting to the world, "What are you waiting for? Go ahead! Smell 'em! Why do so few people *actually* smell them?!"

Taste Your Food

A friend of mine is a professional chef, and he confessed, "We chefs are usually the worst at sitting down and enjoying a good meal. We eat fast food all the time."

How tragic. The smell of exquisite food under their noses all day, and they only have time to wolf down a cheap burger in the car on the way home. Correction: They only *make time* to wolf down a cheap burger. It literally only takes about two more minutes to take a deep breath, think about the taste of the food in your mouth, and enjoy it before moving on to your next bite.

Enjoy What You Have and Stop Dreaming about What You Want

You don't have to be rich to begin savoring "the finer things."

When I was a youth minister in Los Angeles, I regularly took my youth group two hours south to the shanty towns of Tijuana. One "poor" man I encountered left an indelible mark on me. His name was Jesús.

He invited me into his home. He was extremely proud of it. He had built it himself out of pallets and tarp. It was about the size of my bedroom. His dirt floor was swept clean. I didn't know you could sweep a dirt floor clean. Clothes were washed and perfectly folded on the shelves he'd built. He introduced me to his two sons, whom he called his "gorditos" (little fat ones). Their clothes were better pressed than mine. Their hair was more neatly combed than mine too. He showed me a bench seat he had taken from a van that he placed outside on his "porch" and told me about the beautiful view of the moon he has from there. Jesús was so proud of the little he had. He had worked hard for it. And he knew how to enjoy it. In our fifteen minutes together, I could feel his passion for life, his love for his family, and his spirit of gratitude. I realized that I was the poor one. He was happier than those who have much, much more and don't take the time to savor it.

You don't have to be rich to live like a king. God has given you people to love and enjoy. He's given you sunsets and moonrises that surpass the world's greatest paintings. And I have tasted grilled burgers that rival the flavor of the world's best steaks. True story. Get intentional about stopping, savoring, and enjoying life as you have it now (not as you would have it be)—especially on Sundays.

3. Don't rest lazily.

Rest is serious business. Leisure isn't just about not working or about filling the time with mindless distractions (although they certainly have their place).

Ironically, when you do it right, leisure and rest take some effort!

A German philosopher, Josef Pieper, wrote a book in 1948 that we need now more than ever: *Leisure: The Basis of Culture*. In the book, he spells out how rest is at the foundation of any thinking, higher culture. If the Romans or ancient Hawaiians had a highly developed culture, it was because at least a portion of their people stopped working regularly enough and for long enough to devote themselves to study, storytelling, and religion. The very word "school" has its roots in the Greek word for relaxation (σχολή), which led to the Latin word *scola* and the English word *school*. Thinking people come from those who have managed to put their work aside.

You've heard the old phrase that "idle hands are the devil's workshop." Pieper points out that it's not laziness but "an inability to be at leisure, that [goes] together with idleness . . . [which is] the restlessness of work-for-work's-sake." An idling car isn't still. It's shaking about without going anywhere. Becoming "idle" isn't the same as resting. Idleness is constantly fidgeting with small and unimportant things. Resting is a deep, intentional dive into life. Pieper continues, "Leisure is a form of that stillness that is necessary preparation for accepting reality."[4] So, do you rest in a way that raises your spirit, or lowers it a few notches? In a way that brings you into touch with

[4] Maria Popova, "Leisure, the Basis of Culture: An Obscure German Philosopher's Timely 1948 Manifesto for Reclaiming Our Human Dignity in a Culture of Workaholism," *Brain Pickings*, accessed September 15, 2020, https://www.brainpickings.org/2015/08/10/leisure-the-basis-of-culture-josef-pieper/.

reality, or separates you from it, dulling your spirit? In a way that brings you into a deeper encounter with other people, or with your phone? All too often when we need rest, we look for the lowest-hanging fruit. Remember, our brains are hardwired to conserve calories so we can survive. On some very real level, we're built for laziness.

That's why, when we need to refuel, we so often opt for clickbait, scroll Twitter or Reddit, or read the news. And since internet marketers aren't concerned about your happiness but about owning your eyeballs so they can sell ad space, clickbait is often geared to grabbing your attention with something upsetting. Something so bad you can't look away. Or at best, something mind-numbingly distracting. That's not the kind of rest that forms the basis of culture or a happy life.

It's your job to guide your heart and mind to things that lift you up and fuel your joy.

What kind of music makes you really happy? Music that's deeply moving and meaningful, or music that's more easily classified as "cool noises"?

What kind of reading fills you with hope? Tweets or actual books?

What type of image fuels your soul? Clickbait or fine art?

You know the answers to those questions, but you also know which is more readily available and easy to consume. Don't be lazy. Don't opt for idleness and clickbait when your soul craves real truth, beauty, and goodness. That kind of rest can be hard work—but after your Sabbath, your spirit will be refreshed and built up, and not dumbed down.

Rule 8: Serve

Have this mind among yourselves, which was in Christ Jesus. —*Philippians 2:5*

TO EXPERIENCE TRUE JOY, your heart has to shift from self-centered to other-centered. No, this isn't a chapter designed to guilt you for not volunteering at your local soup kitchen. (Not that that would be a bad thing!) But this chapter is about something more. It's about transforming your desire, your life goals, and the way you view success. It's about transforming your attitude.

This chapter also holds the biggest irony in this book: the paradox of the cross, the spiritual law that the only way to find joy is to forget your own quest and help others find it. The only way to truly shine is to help others shine. The only way for someone to "fully find himself [is] through a sincere gift of himself."[1]

In short: If you want to really live, you have to lay down your life.

---

[1] Vatican II, *Gaudium et Spes*, §24.

A Message from Omaha Beach

(I also shared this story in my I AM___ video-coaching program.)

I know a woman who visited Omaha Beach in Normandy, France, where the famous D-Day invasion occurred. She met a veteran there she didn't expect to encounter. He had been a Nazi solider on that infamous day, and he told her his story—the terror he felt seeing a massive fleet of ships coming toward the beach, and the moment that changed his life forever.

As the Allied troops gained the upper hand, he had one bullet left in his rifle, and he thought it was the end. A US soldier charged him, and he took aim and shot the solider in the gut.

The solider dropped to his knees and removed his helmet. Then, he rolled onto his back, made the sign of the cross, and died. "It was at that moment," the old man said, "that I realized that Hitler was not God."

He miraculously survived that day and went AWOL from the Nazi army. He was captured and sent to a prison work camp, and perhaps even more miraculously, ended up surviving the war and visiting Normandy seventy-four years later to remember the battle and to honor the solider that changed his life.

I don't know what that soldier's name was. I'll find out someday, on the other side. But I do know this: He was more than a solider. He was a man fully alive. And he became fully alive by laying down his life.

No hero, no inspiration, no saint, no person you've ever looked up to was self-centered. If you'd like to be average, skip this chapter. If you want to live an uncommonly heroic life like that soldier who died on Omaha beach, and with uncommon joy, read on.

Check Your Desires: Don't Let Your Life Be about Success or Money

Self-help books often focus on *your* success. That's not unimportant, but its importance is definitely overrated. What you *really* want is to be happy. Your own success doesn't make you happy.

Happiness is usually always just beyond the reach of the "success obsessed" who place their happiness in their achievements. That's because highly driven people (and I'm one of them) usually find that when they reach a goal, they change the goalposts. They aim for bigger. Better. And there's nothing wrong with that, so long as you're not living under the delusion that getting "there" will make you happy because "there" is always a step ahead of you.

It's like the end of the rainbow. Ever try to stand under one? I have. It disappears or moves ahead when you get to it. The closest I came was in New Mexico. It was amazing. Right there in front of me, I saw a rainbow hit the ground. Ironically, the part of earth bathed in its dazzling, multicolored light was . . . a Dollar Tree store. Turns out, there wasn't a pot of gold at the end of the rainbow. Just a great bargain.

But I digress . . . making your life about your success at the end of the rainbow leads to a "longing loop." You want. You get. You want something new. The heart is a turbulent ocean of longing because it's made for heaven. That's why every goal achieved leads to a new goalpost. If it doesn't ever feel like "enough," it's because it's not.

Highly driven cultures, where unimaginable worldly success is actually possible, aren't happier than others. Maybe less so. Silicon Valley and Beverly Hills aren't filled with as many smiling faces as Duverger, Haiti, or Cebu, Philippines. I know because I've been there.

Being joyful makes you more likely to succeed with the opportunities you've been given. Not the other way around. That's a well-documented fact—225 studies in the *Psychological Bulletin* found that success doesn't make you happy. Being happy sets you up for success.[2]

Lots and lots of money doesn't make you happier, either. While a certain baseline of money can increase happiness—because it takes you to a place of general safety and security—once your basic needs are covered, it does zero to increase your joy. Nada.[3] Exhaustive studies have even found that lotto winners, while more satisfied and comfortable (obviously), aren't any happier than before they won the lotto. Not even a little tiny bit happier.[4]

---

[2] Shawn Achor, "Positive Intelligence," *Harvard Business Review*, January–February 2012, https://hbr.org/2012/01/positive-intelligence; see also Christy Matta, "Does Success Lead to Happiness," *Psych Central*, July 8, 2018, https://psychcentral.com/blog/does-success-lead-to-happiness/.

[3] Larry Alton, "How Much Money Do You Need to Be Happy?," *Inc.*, June 1, 2018, https://www.inc.com/larry-alton/how-much-money-do-you-need-to-be-happy.html.

[4] Gina Martinez, "Everything You Know about the Fate of Lottery Winners Is Probably Wrong, According to Science," *Time*, October 18, 2018, https://time.com/5427275/lottery-winning-happiness-debunked/.

I can buy more sushi and good sake than when I was twenty-three. I enjoy it. But enjoyment isn't the same thing as joy. I'm not a happier person now that I can occasionally afford sushi than when I was twenty-three years old and the most I could afford was a burger and a cheap beer with friends. Or rather, if I am happier, it's not the sushi that's made me that way. That's true of your life too. Your "stuff" makes you more comfortable, but not happier.

> "God loves a cheerful giver."
> —2 Corinthians 9:7

I'm not knocking the finer pleasures of life. In fact, I think God delights when you delight in his gifts. It's why he gave them to you. But, if you think your joy depends on the things you enjoy, you'll ruin those gifts. You'll cling to them with a desperation that makes them impossible to really enjoy. That's why wealthy people with the wrong hearts are so miserable. What sad irony.

If things like money and power could buy happiness, then successful people would consistently be the happiest people in the office. The further you move from the doorman to the penthouse office, the happier people would be. But we all know that the happiest person is often the receptionist, while the boss is the guy most people want to steer clear of. According to one sad study, 57 percent of employees left their job because of their manager, while an additional 32 percent who stuck around thought about leaving because of him or her. That's a lot of people who don't want to be near the most successful guy in the building.[5]

I'm probably not telling you anything new. You've heard the phrase that money can't buy happiness. Nor can success. So, let me bring this from a reflection to a challenge: Stop wanting it so much! 80 percent of people go through life convinced that more achievement, which they usually quantify as more money, equals more happiness.[6] And because you're "people," you're probably one of them. Stop being one of them! Stop letting your heart believe the lie that happiness lies in more success, more notoriety, more stuff, or more zeros in your bank account. Stop digging for your treasure in the wrong place.

Scripture asks in Isaiah 55:2, "Why do you . . . labor for that which does not satisfy?"

Start speaking truth to yourself. Get in the driver's seat of your own heart. Stop willing things without actually wanting to. Your heart is beautiful and powerful, but it's also dumb. Don't follow your heart. It's all drive, no thought. The heart is a team of horses. But it needs a bit and bridle, or it'll drag you into nowhere-land.

Making life about you and what you achieve and how much you get doesn't work! Only the path of the cross, the path of a soldier on Omaha beach does.

Jesus's first question to humanity in the Gospel of John is "What do you seek?" (John 1:38). He wants to wake us up to what's going on inside our hearts. Are

---

5 "New DDI Research: 57 Percent of Employees Quit Because of Their Boss," *PR Newswire*, December 9, 2019, https://www.prnewswire.com/news-releases/new-ddi-research-57-percent-of-employees-quit-because-of-their-boss-300971506.html.

6 Alton, "How Much Money Do You Need to Be Happy?," *Inc.*

you the boss of your longing? Or do you go through life with unchecked longing for that house/yacht/job/money/achievement, because you're convinced it'll bring you joy when you know it won't?

Your heart is longing for those things because it thinks it's going to find happiness there. But that would be as dumb as your heart pining for a pile of rocks.

"Why do you long for those rocks, oh my heart?"

"Because it will make me happy!" your heart says in reply.

Most people aren't quiet enough to reflect on what longings are guiding their lives, and if they're the right longings or not. You need to be different than "most people." Be aware of your longing, and then let your intellect tell your longing where to go. You need to be aware of your longing and take action to direct it, or in your quest for joy, you'll end up miserable.

Service corrects and directs our desires.

SERVICE IS A REMEDY FOR YOUR MISERY

Maslow came up with the famous hierarchy of needs—his psychological pyramid that culminates in "self-actualization." What most people don't know is that, toward the end of his life, he realized that there's something even higher than self-actualization, and that's self-transcendence.[7]

---

[7] John Messerly, "Summary of Maslow on Self-Transcendence," *Reason and Meaning* (blog), January 18, 2017, https://reasonandmeaning.com/2017/01/18/summary-of-maslow-on-self-transcendence/.

You can only reach that kind of next-level joy by making life about more than just you. And no matter how hard your life is right now, and no matter how many limitations you suffer, you can begin to experience the joy of reaching out beyond yourself through service.

Blessed Chiara Badano, a saintly teen who died of cancer at age eighteen, used to walk around the hospital in pain from the growth on her spine to counsel depressed patients. When she was told to rest, she'd reply, "I'll have time to rest later." When she could no longer walk, she said, "See, I have nothing left, but I still have my heart, and with that I can still love." If you look at her picture, you can see the mind-bending joy on her face as she lay on her deathbed. No matter where you are at in life, you can tap into the joy of service.[8]

[8] To learn more about this joyful woman, visit ChiaraBadano.org

Mother Teresa once told the story of giving a bowl of rice to a poor family. They set one half aside and ate the other. When she encouraged them to eat it all, they told her the other half was for their neighbors. The saintliness hidden in the slums of the world is staggering.

I got to preach when I was in Haiti. It's humbling to preach to a crowd whose lives are so much harder than mine, and whose hearts are so much stronger. I told them, to loud "Amens," to find someone with less than you and help them out. I told them that there's always someone who needs more than you, and God is giving you something so you can give it to them. Whenever you do that, you become rich inside. You are as wealthy as any philanthropist out there. When you give, you have a spirit of abundance, of wealth, of royalty, no matter how poor you are. You become the rich one. Anne Frank said, "No one has ever become poor by giving." To the contrary, our hearts grow rich.

> "We are not looking for a shallow joy but rather a joy that comes from faith, that grows through unselfish love. . . . We realize that joy is demanding; it demands unselfishness." —John Paul II

And that doesn't just apply to money and food but to time and attention. When you're in pain in some way, get out of your head and serve someone else. Are you lonely? Pick up the phone and call a friend who's lonelier than you. Are you obsessing on bad breaks in your life? Call somebody who's had a harder road than you. Encourage them. Are you broke? Help somebody out who's more broke than you. It'll lift you up. And it'll give you some dose of perspective.

God chose to need us. He chose to rely on us. That's because, while he could serve all of humanity's needs all by himself, he wanted to share his joy with us—a joy we can only experience as we love and serve others.

Lose your life and you'll find it again. Try to save your life and you'll lose it (see Matt 16:25). That's the path of Jesus Christ. That's the way of the cross.

DIE! DIE! DIE!

. . . Okay. Maybe that section title is a bit dramatic. But so were Jesus's words to his disciples.

"Take up your cross and follow me," he said (see Matt 16:24). That statement doesn't shake us to our core like it should. Two thousand years after the age of crucifixions and we've sterilized the cross, but to give you some context, if he'd said that today, he would have said, "Sit in your electric chair and follow me." That's how disturbing that phrase sounded in first-century Palestinian ears. DIE! And I promise, you'll find the life you were made for. But only if you die to yourself.

I'm not saying you should kill your dreams. Go ahead. Achieve! Conquer! Succeed! Thrive! But if you want to be happy doing all that, don't make it about you.

As the joyful Paul wrote to the Philippians from chains, "Have this mind among yourselves, which was in Christ Jesus" (Phil 2:5). Paul is inviting us to trade in our rusty old patterns of thinking for a new mind. Our old minds evolved to obsess on self-preservation, "but we have the mind of Christ" (1 Cor 2:16). Paul continues, "Though he was in the form of God, [Christ] did not count equality with God a thing to be grasped, but emptied himself, taking the form of a servant" (Phil 2:6–7).

Paul isn't just exhorting us to do "service-y" things. He wants you to think like a servant. He doesn't want you to do the dishes with a chip on your shoulder. He doesn't want you to mow the lawn like you're doing the world a favor. He doesn't want you to polish your halo before you serve the poor. He wants you to consider yourself a servant just doing his job. As Jesus says, "When you have done all that is commanded you, say, 'We are unworthy servants; we have only done what was our duty'" (Luke 17:10). Those sound like harsh words, but Jesus spoke them because he wants your joy to be complete. And if you don't put on the mind of a servant, you can't have joy.

THE SECRET PATH TO JOY

Taking on the mind of a servant doesn't only make you holier; it makes you happier. It doesn't only unlock your potential as a human being. It releases a flood of joy into your soul. I see this principle play out in my own life constantly.

I had a fight with my wife recently. I went to prayer after this fight and complained to God, "Lord, does it always have to be about her? Why can't it be about me? I mean, really, why can't I have my needs met? Why do I always have to care about her needs?" (It was a very mature prayer. Not.)

God spoke to me in that moment, not with an audible voice, but an unmistakable spiritual voice that wasn't my own broke into my consciousness. He said, "Yes, Chris, it *can* be all about you. You have every right to make it about you, about your needs, about your interests, and to forget about her and her needs. You have every right to not live an extraordinary life. You have every right to be an average and ordinary man. You have every right to not become a saint." "Okay, Lord. I withdraw my prayer." Joy returned to me in that moment. And sanity.

It's the paradox of the cross that when we lose ourselves, we find ourselves. The days I wake up and think, "My wife is lacking these five qualities of a perfect spouse. I should tell her!"—those are not my best days.

The days I wake up and think, "How can I make my wife the happiest wife in the world today?" I end up being the happiest husband in the world. Go figure!

How-To

So, how do you "meta your noia" into the mind of a servant so that you can live with deeper freedom and joy? How do you turn that mind of yours, forged in the fires of millions of years of evolution to obsess about self-preservation, into a mind that embraces the cross? Here's three simple (as always) tips:

1. Claim it. Out loud.

I'm a fan of articulating truths to yourself as a part of

your day. Remember, God didn't reveal his truth to you so you'd wait for me to preach to you. You need to preach to yourself. Out loud.

My friend Justin is a very busy man. He's a loving dad of nine children. (Catholic? Yes.) He owns more than one business. And he generally kicks butt at life. But I think the key to his happiness (and success) lies in the way he mentally sets the course for his day. When he wakes up, and before he hits the day, he falls to his knees, kisses the floor, and says one word in Latin: *Serviam*.

In Catholic tradition, Lucifer, which means "light bringer," was the most beautiful of angels, but his fall, and the fall of the countless angels he brought with him, was brought about by his battle cry of *Non serviam*! "I will not serve!" And so he became a demon, no longer a light bringer but the embodiment of light's absence. Justin says, "I want my motto to be the opposite of Satan's motto. *Serviam*. I will serve."

When we take on the mind of a servant, we become a source of light. We shine like the sun into every place we go. When our lives repeat the motto of the dark angels, we become the opposite of a sun. Spiritually, we become black holes. A black hole is nothing more than a star that's collapsed in on itself. All its potential and potency is turned within. Eventually, its gravitational pull inward becomes so intense that not even light from nearby stars can escape it, and astronomers know it's there when they discover a funnel of light getting sucked from a nearby star into nothing.

When you walk into a room and you're having "one of those days," you suck the light out of everyone.

Sometimes you have your own "event horizon" around you, and people know they need to steer clear. You might not be able to shift your mood easily in those moments, but that's okay. Your mood doesn't matter as much as your will. Say it out loud, *serviam*, and begin to shift your thinking.

2. Don't just sit there. Do something.

You need to contribute to be happy.

An old friend of mine once told me, "I have nothing to give." Tragically, he ended his life a week after he said those words. That is a lie from the pit of hell. Never give permission or power to that lie.

Everyone can give something. So, where to start?

Serve the Poor

If you want to throw your life away, do it in the slums of a distant land serving the poor. Don't do it with heroin or suicide. Ironically, if you throw your life away in the slums of a distant land, you'll probably find it.

I've been to the poorest places on earth. I've met orphans in places that are overrun with parentless children. It's amazing how much they just want to be held. Feel like you have nothing to give? Can you hold an orphan? Then you have something to give. Can you serve in a food line in your city and make eye contact and smile at the homeless whose greatest pain is feeling "invisible"? Then you have something to give. And you need to give that something.

You need to do *something* to serve the poor. For your

own sake. Not just the spiritually poor. The literally poor. Read Matthew 25. It's the cheat sheet for "the final exam." Whatever you did for them, you did for Jesus. Whatever you didn't do for them, you failed to do for God himself. I don't know what that looks like for you, but I do know your salvation depends on you finding a good answer to that question. (I know, I know: Jesus saves, and we can't earn that. But the Jesus who saves was clear on multiple occasions that he doesn't want to save us if we don't want to serve those in need.) I think that is, in no small part, because of the kind of people we become when we open our eyes to and serve people in need, and the kind of people we become when we don't. For the self-focused, hell begins here and now. We've all experienced this.

Our nonprofit, Real Life Catholic, does a lot to partner with other organizations in serving the needy. Thanks to our donors, we give to our partner organizations in a big way. And every time they thank me, I thank them for giving me and our supporters an opportunity to save our own souls. We need the poor more than they need us. Serving them turns me outside of myself and cleanses me of the worldly cling-ons that attach to my soul and make me miserable.

You don't have to become Mother Teresa. You just have to do your part, even if it's as small as giving monthly to an organization that serves the poor. A little goes a long way for your joy, and a little from everyone goes a long way for the poor.

Remember: Little Acts of Service Are a Big Deal

We often think "I'm just small and insignificant, what can I do? I don't have a nonprofit or a stage or even write books. I'm not rich. I'm not famous," and so we do nothing. After all, we're not "big deals," and those small acts of love and service aren't that big of a deal. Right? Wrong.

Friends, there are two billion Christians walking this earth today. What if we all stopped saying "What can I do" and started asking, with an open heart, "What can I do?" The world would change if all of us did our "little something."

Start with the opportunities right under your nose and stop overlooking their importance. Everything from holding the door open for the person who annoys you to the small act of evangelization of saying "God bless you" to the person who gave you coffee—it all makes a difference. It all blankets the world with the love of God.

We underestimate our impact because we weigh things with the wrong scales.

We only see life in one dimension. We only see the here and now. But when we stand before God at the end of time, outside of time, we'll see that our "stage" spans the millennia. We'll see the ripple effect of all the little things we've done.

From the eternal point of view, a man you never heard of named Jan Tyranowski brought down Communism in eastern Europe and impacted millions of lives with the power of the Gospel. He's probably why you're reading this book right now.

Jan lived in a small town in Poland while the Nazis and then Communists took over. He couldn't do much, but to keep the Faith and his culture alive, he started a small group to help a few young men keep their faith through those hard times. They'd meet, share life, and pray the rosary. Then Jan died, unnoticed by the world.

One of the men in his small group went on to become Pope John Paul II, who changed the world, and my life personally. You never know your impact.

My son is an Army combat medic and a man of deep faith. He's driven by the idea that if he saves one life, in a thousand years that's thousands of lives who may not have gotten the chance to live.

Don't just look at the here and now. Know that each act of love and service ripples to the end of time. Each concrete act of love is of infinite importance.

3. Give money away.

It's been said that money can't buy happiness. That's not true. It's a scientifically proven fact that money can, in fact, make you happy, but only when you spend it on other people!

One study of 632 Americans asked how much they earned and asked them to rate their own happiness. The results: income level didn't matter. Those who spend money on themselves weren't happier. Those who gave it away were. In a second study, a group of employees was given a large bonus and a few months later asked how they spent it and how it impacted their happiness. There was a direct correlation between an increase in happiness and how much the person had spent on charity.[9]

Jesus said, "It is more blessed to give than to receive" (Acts 20:35). Turns out, once again, the science backs Jesus.

I give monthly to several charities (including my own Real Life Catholic). It's addictive. I also try to be open to opportunities to give a little extra when I'm able. I'm not rich, so I don't give a ton away, but I do give what I can, and I do cash out on a lot of joy.

Winston Churchill once said, "We make a living by what we get. We make a life by what we give."

BE AN ANSWER TO PRAYER

When we give, we can have the joy of being God's answer to someone's prayer. I was in a hotel in the Deep South, and I heard a woman who was working at the hotel kitchen say to her coworker, "Lord, I'd be so blessed if I could have one of these waffle makers to bring home for my grandkids." When I was back in my hotel room, I called my wife and shared how beautiful black Southern culture is, how sacred words like "Lord" and "blessed" flow so naturally in the course of their conversations. And I remarked on how many blessings, like our waffle maker, we take for granted.

My wife was horrified that I was merely inspired rather than spurred to action. "Are you crazy? Get her a waffle maker! Duh!" I went and found out how to get

[9]   James Randerson, "The Path to Happiness: It Is Better to Give Than Receive," *The Guardian*, March 21, 2008, https://www.theguardian.com/science/2008/mar/21/medicalresearch.usa.

her a package and ordered the best waffle maker I could afford. She'll never know who did that, but she'll know her prayer was answered. It felt great.

God answers prayers through us—big and small—when we listen to him, and the people around us (and our wives). And, at the same time, he answers our deepest prayer for joy.

Rule 9:
Frame Your
Mind with Faith

*Set your mind on things that are above, not
on things that are on earth.* —*Colossians 3:2*

YOU'VE HEARD THE PHRASE, "frame of mind." Your frame of mind isn't what you're thinking. Your frame of mind is where you're thinking from. It's the headspace wherein your thoughts happen. Most of us approach everyday life without taking ownership of our frame of mind. By default, we let our circumstances or our passing moods frame our thinking rather than what we *want* to have frame it.

The most powerful, joy-inducing "frame" your mind can have is formed by your faith.

Faith isn't only *religious practice*. Faith is the way

you see everything. It's how you answer life's big questions. It's the frame that shapes your "big picture" for life. If that frame is fundamentally bad, good times are just a distraction. If that frame is a cause for joy, your life can be joyful even when it's difficult.

But you need to be intentional about your faith framing your mind for it to make that kind of difference in your life. Let's dive into exactly how to do that, or rather, how to allow God's grace to do that in you!

THE POWER OF A FRAME

Phil Braun has been on the other side of the camera for most of the things I've filmed. From the Chosen Confirmation program, which, thank God, has helped form a million people preparing for Confirmation, to risking his fingers and toes while he stood in Lake Michigan during a blizzard to film me attempting to surf on our reality show, *Real Life Catholic*—he's always there. And he's great at what he does.

I asked him how he landed on his chosen career. He said, "I discovered that I'm just really good at seeing the world through a box. I'm good at putting a frame around things." What an elegantly simple summary of everything from fine art, to photography, to film.

Artists, photographers, and videographers select one spot in a panorama, put a rectangular frame around it, and share it with the world. Bad art, like bad photojournalism, slaps a frame on reality that creates tunnel vision and pushes an agenda, blinding you to reality.

I'll never forget taking part in a peaceful pro-life

march as a young man. A photojournalist elbowed past me and the throng of young people in the march to an old woman marching with us. She lifted her camera high, aimed it down at her so as to cut us out of the picture, and captured the picture of a lone grandma, rosary in hand, marching for life. Some framing hides reality.

Good framing doesn't do that. On one hand, it presents a picture that's smaller than the panorama, and on the other, it opens your heart and mind to a larger reality. The picture of a butterfly landing on a small wildflower at the base of a mountain opens you up to a new way of seeing the entire mountain range. The photo of a kid laughing and playing in a fire hydrant in the midst of a busy cityscape helps you see all of New York City differently.

Your mind has a frame that you see everything through. You're usually not aware that it's there, but like it or not, it impacts how you experience everything.

The Frame Makes the Picture

If you're in a defensive frame of mind today, you'll respond to a coworker's suggestion differently than if you feel safe and confident. If your teen is in an angry state of mind, he'll process your request to do the dishes far differently than if he feels loved and happy.

Frame of mind doesn't just determine what we think but how we think. Studies confirming this fact have come to shape everything from hostage negotiation tactics to the art of sealing a deal taught in the top business schools.

Hostage negotiators used to rely on the art of logic.

If a terrorist is holding hostages, surely you can reason with him, ask what he wants, and come to an amenable agreement that gets him and his hostages out in a way that minimizes harm and maximizes gain for all parties involved, right? Wrong. After countless failures, negotiators learned that in any hostage situation, life and death depend on managing someone's frame of mind more than managing the exchange of information.

A terrorist who is offered a good deal and who feels relaxed and safe and trusts the hostage negotiator results in lives saved. An on-edge terrorist who feels that he is being taken advantage of and disrespected with the same exact good deal results in dead hostages. It's as simple as that.

The discoveries of hostage negotiators have influenced top business schools around the world. Negotiations, it turns out, don't happen by logically strong-arming people with an airtight case and an irrefutable PowerPoint.

In his book, *Never Split the Difference,* former FBI hostage negotiator turned business guru, Chris Voss, observes that man

> has two systems of thought: System 1, our animal mind, is fast, instinctive, and emotional; System 2 is slow, deliberative, and logical. And System 1 is far more influential. In fact, it guides and steers our rational thoughts. System 1's inchoate beliefs, feelings, and impressions are the main sources of the explicit beliefs and deliberate choices of System 2. They're the spring that feeds the river. We react emotionally (System 1)

to a suggestion or question. Then that System 1 reaction informs and in effect creates the System 2 answer.[1]

In other words, your frame of mind—shaped by beliefs you often don't know you have or aren't paying attention to, feelings you didn't choose, and gut-level responses you're unaware of—has a powerful part in shaping what you *think* are purely logical conclusions.

One extreme and tragic example of this can be seen in wilderness survival situations. It's a well-known fact that the number one killer in the wild isn't cold, hunger, or thirst. It's panic. Once you panic, your mind is no longer looking for what it needs to survive. It just wants you to run and hide. There are stories of people, lost in a blizzard, who gave into panic so profoundly that their minds unraveled into paranoia.

One man was found hiding, frozen to death, right near where rescuers had passed by calling his name. Terror took over his System 1 thinking so powerfully that it overrode his System 2 conclusions. Everything was interpreted in the light of terror. Even rescuers were seen as a threat he needed to hide from.

We all approach everyday life with a frame of mind. While the wrong frame of mind doesn't usually lead to our deaths, it does often stop us from really living.

When St. Paul wrote, "Be transformed by the renewal of your mind" (Rom 12:2), he wasn't just exhorting you to learn your faith. To borrow Voss's language,

---

[1] Chris Voss, *Never Split the Difference: Negotiating as If Your Life Depended on It* (New York: HarperCollins, 2016), 12.

Paul wasn't just saying to fill your System 2 thinking with the right logical constructs about God. He was saying to make a shift to your System 1. He was exhorting you to change your frame of mind.

That's what faith does—or at least, that's what faith is *supposed to* do for us. Faith is meant to *be* your frame of mind. It puts a frame on life that, on one hand, focuses your vision, and on the other hand, opens you up to all of reality more fully. You don't just stare at the frame. You look through it at everything else. The Bible is like that.

> "Rejoice in your hope."
> —Romans 12:12

We're not just meant to see the book but, rather, everything through it: God. Purpose. Joy. Pain. Life. Death.

Faith answers our fundamental questions about what the purpose of life is, if we're loved or lovable, whether we're a cosmic accident or really matter at all, what happens when we die; and those answers frame every other thought and experience that enter our consciousness.

When faith plays that mighty of a role in our lives, we begin to experience what it means to be "new creations" (2 Cor 5:17), living life to the full (John 10:10). We begin to experience the joy that Jesus promised when he said that he had come to share the very joy of the Trinity with us (John 15:11), a joy that nothing can take away (John 16:22).

Sadly, most people never get there. Religion remains just a part of the picture. Their mental framing—their worldview—is built by something else. That's why they have faith but not joy. They have a faith that teaches them the God of the universe died for them and they're on a train to glory, but it's just a nice story they believe in—not the story of *their* lives.

The saints are people who let the Faith frame their minds, shaping their hearts on a deep, even subconscious, level.

ST. PAUL'S FRAME OF MIND

Amazingly, most of what St. Paul wrote about joy—how to have the right frame of mind, keeping a great attitude, and living with gratitude—was written from prison while awaiting execution. It's thought that the city sewage ran by his cell in Rome. Picture him sitting there, not only in chains but in stench, and writing, "Rejoice in the Lord always; again I will say, Rejoice" (Phil 4:4).

His miserable circumstances didn't frame his mind. He lived with a constant awareness of the presence of something bigger than his passing circumstances.

In every one of his prison letters, he introduced himself in noble terms, "Paul, an apostle of Jesus Christ" and "Paul, a prisoner of Jesus Christ." Note that he didn't say, "Paul, a prisoner of Rome." That's because, as big as the Roman Empire was back then, there was something even bigger to frame it.

We all go through life with an awareness of "something bigger" that frames our minds. It's how we see life itself, and it shapes how we perceive the experiences that life consists of.

- Do you see life as a tragedy? Maybe a disease taught you to see everything that way.
- Do you see life as a struggle? Maybe deprivation taught you that.
- Do you see it as a trial? Maybe conditional love taught you that.
- Do you see it as an opportunity? Maybe your parents' great worth ethic taught you that.
- Do you see it as a party? Maybe too many eighties movies taught you that.
- Do you see it as a bit of all of the above?

There's a better frame for life than all that.

Paul's prison epistles are dripping with hope, expectation, a sense of dignity and power, and, above all, joy. You'd never guess that Paul wasn't smelling church incense, but city sewage. Paul could have let his circumstances shape his frame of mind, and initially he probably did! That's why he wrote to the Philippians from prison, "I have *learned*, in whatever state I am, to be content" (Phil 4:11). But eventually he wrote, "Set your minds on things that are above" (Col 3:2).

So, what is the "something bigger" that framed Paul's mind and shaped his thinking? Let's look at a modern-day saint that I met in an unexpected place for the answer.

JOHN SIMONE'S FRAME OF MIND

I went to Haiti on a mission trip to film for our show, *Real Life Catholic*. Our mission was in a poor part of

Haiti. If you're familiar with Haiti, you know that's saying a lot. We were probably an hour from the nearest paved road. The Industrial Revolution seemed to skip over the place we were. And there, thousands of miles from home and a few hundred years removed from the rest of the world, I met a man I'll never forget. His name is John Simone.

John had been in an accident that left him mostly paralyzed from the neck down—though he had enough nerve endings alive to feel some pain. His village had hated him because he had been a gangster, so they left him to literally rot.

When the missionaries found him, his bedsores were so bad that his ribcage and spine were exposed. His bed was sagging to the ground from his own feces. John's nine-year-old son had kept him alive with what scraps of food he could find and with bug spray for John's gaping sores. (Poverty in America is real, but poverty in Haiti is something that's hard to wrap your brain around until you've seen it.)

Through their care of him, the missionaries saved his life and brought him into a relationship with God. I joined them to care for John's bedsores, and as I approached the house he never leaves, which was smaller than my bedroom, I didn't know what to expect. What I saw shocked me.

A smile. And not just any smile. It was literally the most beaming smile I had ever seen in my life.

I don't smile as big as John when I'm "struggling" with Denver traffic. I, who had come to help him, was quickly humbled in the presence of this giant soul. His little hut in a remote jungle in Haiti suddenly felt like a cathedral towering over me.

I cared for John's bedsores. I thanked him for his faith. I felt so connected to the man that I kissed his forehead like he was my brother—because he is my brother. I asked, "How do you keep your spirits so high?" He said, "I think of other things." What "other things?" What distractions could possibly be larger than his dire circumstances? The answer was painted over his bed: an image of Jesus and Mary on the ceiling he looked at all day. And John didn't just spend most of his time staring "at" that painting; he saw his life through it.

John is a saint. And saints have a joy that can't be

conquered. John was like St. Paul, who wrote beautiful phrases like, "In all these things we are *more* than conquerors" (Rom 8:37).

So, what is it about the mental framing of this faith that gave John such inexplicable joy? In a word: Love. Nothing makes us happier than love, and Christian faith reveals that the right frame for all of life, every interaction, and everything that happens to us, is love.

FRAMED BY LOVE

Love and Happiness

We're made for love. Love brings us into existence. I told my son about the birds and the bees, and he asked, "Is there any other way?" There's not. God has chosen to make the breath of life contingent on the act of love.

Love is the source of life. That's why *falling in love*, and *being fallen in love with*, is the most happiness-making experience in life. (It's also why broken experiences of love are among the most devastating.)

My daughter was recently married. There's a reason the Bible calls heaven a wedding feast. A holy wedding is the most joy-inducing experience in life. There's a smile, and then there's the "bride at the end of the aisle" kind of smile. It's otherworldly. We love love more than anything else because it makes us more joyful than anything else.

I was slightly out of my mind with joy when I started dating my wife. I didn't think straight. It hurt my grades at college. It was worth it. (And Dr. Scott Hahn, my thesis advisor, was very merciful with me!) Our joy-seeking souls are driven to love when we find it. We can't help it. And when we look for it in the wrong places, it drives us off a cliff. Many of life's worst choices are driven by a misguided quest for love. When men think they'll find what only love can give through accomplishments, they become workaholics; when women think they'll find it at the wrong club, they might get used; when teens think they'll find love and acceptance with that group of pot smokers, they become addicts. We give everything to purchase love because we crave the joy love promises. When we find love, it's worth every penny. When we look in the wrong places, it robs us blind.

But in the end, the ultimate love isn't "out there," around the next bend, in that next boyfriend, or even in "the perfect marriage" (which doesn't exist). The love that has the power to take up every tattered page of your life and make it part of a love story—framing all of existence in something "far more [abundant] than all that we ask or think" (Eph 3:20)—is only found in Faith. And more specifically, Christian faith.

God Is Love

The *God who is Love* presented to us in the Bible isn't just a nicer, mythological creature to replace the gods of old. He's not a mighty man flying around in space, only loving instead of mean. He is utterly beyond what mankind had previously meant by the word "God." The gods of the ancients were characters in the story of human existence. Zeus was really powerful. He wasn't "all powerful." He was knowing. He wasn't "all knowing."

He existed. He wasn't "I Am." He wasn't "Existence It-self." He wasn't any bigger than the story. He was just a big guy in it.

The gods of the ancients were like Gandalf, showing up from time to time to help the hobbits out. The God of Christianity is like J. R. R. Tolkien, the author him-self, showing up on page 162. That doesn't change the story line. It changes the whole story.[2] We are not living in a story where Love shows up to help us out. We're living in a Love Story. We are living *in* God. That is the Christian worldview. That's the lens through which we read every page of the Bible and experience every page of life.

When you find the love that is God, you've found the "something bigger" that Paul knew in prison. If your life were a story, the title

> "Joy is the infallible sign of the presence of God."
> —Pierre Teilhard de Chardin

would not be "divorce," "abuse," "disease," or "failure." (Failure isn't a person; it's an event.) Those are all just pages in a bigger story. Of course, we who are in Christ live and die just like everyone else. And most of the pages of life look the same at a glance, but if you step back, you'll see a different story. A new cover binds all the pages together. It's a love story. And because of that, we have joy.

I say this without apology: faith in Jesus Christ of-fers the best possible "framing" for life ever proposed by anyone. In fact, for all the bad press the Church has

---

[2] Peter Kreeft makes a similar point. See *Jesus-Shock* (South Bend, IN: St. Augustine's Press), 41. I highly recommend this book!

earned in recent years, and for all the failings of his followers, it's still the case that nothing even comes close to the message of Jesus Christ when it comes to a joy-inducing, uplifting way to experience your own existence.

An atheistic worldview can't offer you what Jesus does. A Godless frame of mind is totally empty. An atheistic worldview is a string of events without a story. If there's no author, there's no story. If there's no God, then any meaning you find in life is meaning you made up, which is make-believe, which isn't "real." If there's no God, you are no more than a lucky lump of self-aware molecules that emerged from a universe and shouldn't be here and someday won't be. Eventually, all the stars will go out, and the universe will implode, or rip to shreds, or (insert your doomsday scenario here). The end. If you meet an atheist with joy and hope, in the words of my friend Kenn Hensley, ask him to show you his receipt, because joy and hope are not consistent with what he thinks about our existence.

A vaguely spiritual worldview can't give you what Jesus can, either. People who claim to be "spiritual but not religious" have traded in the image of a personal, loving God for an amorphous force. (Maybe it's because a vague force has no demands on us and enables us to stay our own little gods?) They mistake "vague" for "profound." As if a God who preferred to stay hidden behind the clouds is profound? It's not. Or maybe they replace the word "God" with the word "universe." I hate to break it to you: nature doesn't care about you. Just ask the coronavirus.

Faith in the "wrong" god can't bring you what Jesus can, either. A vision of God who doesn't really love me and who didn't enter my world to suffer for me and with me is a cold religion in the end. While I respect other faiths, I can't imagine God being anything less than the love that would enter this human mess with me.

Only the One who is Love can turn all of life into a love story—and a good one. That's why only he can give you the joy you're looking for. In the words of Pope Benedict XVI, "The happiness you are seeking, the happiness you have a right to enjoy, has a name and a face: it is Jesus of Nazareth."[3]

Anchored in Love

My friend Lizz, who died of cancer, and her husband Ryan, whom she left behind with their four small children, shared the tattoo of an anchor. It's not just because she was in the Coast Guard. It's because they're Catholic Christians. In first-century churches in Rome, you can see anchors carved into the walls. It's a symbol of hope. For the first Christians, persecution was regular and gruesome. Your friends and family were often fed to lions in the Colosseum. The last sound they heard was the applause of their neighbors. Bloodbaths were a part of life. Christians were impaled, covered in tar, and lit on fire to keep the emperor Nero's palace lit at night. Strangely, Christians were also joyful. The writings of Church leaders at that time weren't obsessed

---

[3] Benedict XVI, Address at the Poller Rheinwiesen Wharf, August 18, 2005, in *L'Osservatore Romano*, August 24, 2005, 4.

with the politics of Rome. They were too busy being excited about what God was doing to be obsessed with what the emperor was doing.

The choppy surface of the sea doesn't disturb an anchor. Hurricanes and tidal waves and persecutions and job loss and cancer and (insert your waves here) can't rob you of your hope when it's anchored in the Love that is God. The tattered pages of your life can't rob you of your sense of story when they're bound by the Gospel. And that's why all the things life throws at us can make us sad on the natural level, but they can't rob the deeper, spiritual joy in a Christian soul.

Jesus promised, "No one will take your joy from you" (John 16:22), because the world can't take what it didn't give you.

For this reason, Rule 9 is the rule for a joyful life that lasts when all others fade. It's a light when all other lights go out. And when you can't control the other rules for a joyful life (which you won't always be able to, especially as you approach your own death someday), it only makes Rule 9 stronger in your heart. When you can't engage your body in the battle for joy because it fails you, you can make your body an offering to the Lord. When you can't achieve any balance because you have no idea what tomorrow will bring, you can know the Lord has a plan for your life—be it a long or short life. When you can't think of what to give thanks for, you can thank God for loving you. Framing your mind in the Faith is the unconquerable source of joy. No, not the shallower feeling of passing happiness, nor the denial of pain, which is real, but the awareness of something beyond pain's reach.

As Sam and Frodo approached Mount Doom in the *Lord of the Rings*, just when all hope was about to fade, Sam looked up, beyond his dire circumstances, to something untouched and untouchable by the world:

> There, peeping among the cloud-wrack above a dark tor high up in the mountains, Sam saw a white star twinkle for a while. The beauty of it smote his heart, as he looked up out of the forsaken land, and hope returned to him. For like a shaft, clear and cold, the thought pierced him that in the end the Shadow was only a small and passing thing: there was light and high beauty for ever beyond its reach.[4]

St. Paul had joy as he approached his death, because his mind was framed by a high beauty beyond death's reach.

John Simone had joy as he lay in his bed, unable to move, because his thinking wasn't framed by the reality of his paralysis but by the reality of his freedom as a beloved child of God.

My father had a sense of humor as he lay on what he thought was his deathbed a year ago, because in the moment he was a man facing not death but Life itself.

And *that* is redemption. Being freed from sin is just a small part of what redemption is all about. A truly redeemed soul is redeemed from everything, redeemed by the joy and the hope of the Gospel. The waves of life might crash down, but we've learned to surf.

---

[4] J. R. R. Tolkien, *The Return of the King: Being the Third Part of the Lord of the Rings* (New York: Ballantine Books, 1965), 211.

That's what the light of Christian faith does for us in the here and now. And keeping your mind on the stuff of eternity while you stroll through the valley of the shadow of death isn't just the rule for when all else fails. It's also the rule that helps you live out and enjoy the others most fully! Everything from gratitude, to silence, to rest, to engaging your body, to friendship—it all takes on a fuller dimension when it's framed in the worldview of the Gospel. All these things are to be experienced not as the result of luck but the gift of Love.

But how do you make the leap from having faith to faith having you? How do you shift faith from merely System 2 to System 1? How do you go from letting it be a part of the panorama to making up your *frame of mind*?

How-To

1. Reject toxic faith. Receive Love.

Most people in the ancient world grew up with the idea that God is very, very angry.

The pagans of old believed in the divine enough to have a meaningful story for life, but it wasn't necessarily a good one. For the most part, the gods of the ancients were jerks. They were like you on your worst day, only, look out, dad can throw lightning bolts at the kids when he comes home from work. People in the ancient world may have been happy, but it was despite their faith, not because of it. Zeus is simply not happy making. He's fear inducing.

It's worth noting that some Christians still see God that way, but that's not real Christianity. They're doing it wrong. They think God's default is to be angry with us, that if he "loves" us, it's because that's his job, but he doesn't like us. In fact, he can't stand us. That kind of religion replaces healthy guilt with toxic shame, relationship with rules, and love with fear. A person who approaches God that way will obey him, and even get to heaven, but he probably won't take anyone with him, and when he gets there, he'll kick himself for living such an unnecessarily joyless life!

The truth of the Gospel is that you don't earn the love of God any more than an infant earns the love of its mother. In fact, in the Bible, God makes it clear that he loves us even more than our mothers: "Can a woman forget her sucking child, that she should have no compassion on the son of her womb? Even these may forget, yet I will not forget you. Behold, I have graven you on the palms of my hands" (Isa 49:15–16).

Like a good parent, God doesn't love you because of who you are but because of who he is. He can't help but love you. And you couldn't earn that love if you tried. If you think your sins make you unworthy of his love, remember that he loves you because it's an act worthy of him!

When you mess up, don't think of yourself as "messed up." Think of yourself as a beloved child of God whom he loved enough to DIE for (what more could God do to prove that he loves you?) who just made a mistake.

I'm not saying that obedience to God is unimportant. I'm saying that that's not what makes him love you. Jesus said, "If you love me, you will keep my commandments" (John 14:15). If I might sum up the condemned heresy of Jansenism, it twists those words to: "If you keep my commands, I will love you." That's not what Jesus said. You aren't loved on a conditional-love basis with God. That's not Christianity. That's a spiritual slavery that Jesus set us free from.

You might be reading this and thinking, "But Chris, you don't know what *my* sin is. My sin is far too big . . ." For what? The *Maker of the Universe*!? Haha! (Sorry for laughing at you. I just think that's funny.)

I met someone on a trip recently. She came up to me with a little baby in her arms and said, "This baby is because of your event here last year." Obviously, that caught me off guard! But she continued, "I had had an abortion in high school, and I felt like I was damned. After hearing the message of the Gospel, I realized that I was redeemable and that God's love tells me who I am. I'm not my past mistakes. I'm his daughter."

She got right with God, and made a good confession. And she and her husband decided to have a baby shortly thereafter. A toxic faith would have had her hiding from God the rest of her life. People blame the Church for that kind of faith, but I've rarely heard a condemning preacher yelling at people from the pulpit. More often, it's the "accuser of our brethren" (Rev 12:10) whispering in our hearts after we sin, especially if we "dare" to enter a church.

But whatever the source, removing this toxin is simple:

1. It starts with me calling it out and recognizing it in your heart. When you see something that's making you miserable, your soul begins to reject it like your stomach might reject rancid meat.

And

2. Practice resting in his love for you.

I want you to do something very powerful that only takes a minute, and I want you to do this every day. It's how I kicked off my coaching programs I AM___ (which helps you see yourself through God's eyes), RISE (my men's program), and my own prayer life every single day.

Take a deep breath. Quiet your heart. And picture Jesus looking at you from the cross. He's not looking at the world, just you. Zoom in on his eyes as he lays down his life for you. What do they say to you?

Do that right now for sixty seconds in total silence. (I'm serious. Put down the book and do it.) Don't speak. Just receive. Just let him love you.

Before an infant learns his name, he learns his identity, not by looking in a mirror but by looking at mom and dad. This is the foundation of the Christian life: not what we do for him but receiving what he did for us. "He first loved us" (1 John 4:19).

2. Make a decision for Love.

God declares that "you are loved" with the love that is himself—a love mighty enough to create space and time and passionate enough to conquer death for you.

If we can sum up the entire story of the Bible, and of human existence, it's this: your God is in love with you. Madly in love.

Have you received that love? For you? You didn't earn that love, and you couldn't if you tried. "If a man offered for love all the wealth of his house, it would be utterly scorned" (Song 8:7). Your "stuff" simply can't buy love! This is even more true with the love of God.

So, what's your role in getting what's freely given? It starts here: make a choice for it, and ask for it.

An act of the will is critical when it comes to love. Some people date forever. (Aren't you going to ask her to marry you?!) They go through the motions of life with love at their side, and they never really enter into it.

People approach Christianity this way. They "go through the motions." They know that God gives us his very self in every Communion, but he goes past their hearts and into their stomachs. They know he's Lord of the universe but don't invite him to be Lord of their lives. They confess their sins and know he forgives but don't claim that truth enough to forgive themselves.

I dated my wife for a year and half, but life didn't *really* change until I made a decision, took a knee, and asked a question, and she said yes. God waits for the movement of your will and the opening of your heart. He waits for you to really and truly decide for his love. You can't experience faith really and truly changing your life until you "go there." I'm not asking you to make Christianity a part of the panorama of your life. If you want joy, you need to make it the frame.

"But I don't want to be a religious fanatic!" It's funny

how people aren't afraid to be sports or car or video game or sex fanatics when none of those things can lead to lasting joy! Don't be afraid. Deep faith doesn't make you someone else. It makes you fully *you*. God isn't standing by to rob you of your personality.

Go there with me right now. After spending a minute thinking of God loving you (see #1 above), pray this prayer with me. Pray it daily if you'd like. But let it mean something as you pray it now. I'd encourage you to pen in the date you prayed it on this page:

A Prayer to Receive Jesus into Your Life in a New and Deeper Way

Lord Jesus, You are the love that I was born to find.
You are here, offering ME your heart.
And asking for mine in return.
You have given me the freedom to say no.
I use my freedom to say yes.
I surrender all I am to you.
I renounce Satan. Sin.
The spirit of despair.
And the lie that I am unlovable.
I forgive others, and I forgive myself
of my worst sin.
And I ask you to forgive me and to forgive those
who have hurt me.
You are Lord of the Universe.
Be Lord of my heart.
I say yes to you.

3. Practice your faith.

If someone is active at church, they'll refer to themselves as a "practicing Catholic." I like the word "practicing" because, on one level, it implies "active." But, on another level, it implies "amateur," "messy," and "often failing." And that's okay. The important thing is that we keep practicing, even when it's hard, because, in the words of St. Peter, "Lord, to whom shall we go?" (John 6:68).

I'd love to see the whole world be devout, practicing followers of Jesus Christ. Is that because I want to heap religious burdens on everyone? No. It's because I share the desire of Jesus, and of St. John, to see your joy be complete (see John 15:11; 1 John 1:4).

In the words of St. Pope John Paul II, "It is Jesus ... that you seek when you dream of happiness; he is waiting for you when nothing else you find satisfies you."[5] Joy is the fragrance of God. To have joy is to have God.

He hasn't made himself difficult to find. (What a cruel trick that would be, to have created us to seek him, and then to hide from us!) You don't need to climb a mountain in Tibet. You don't need to learn any mantras. Christianity isn't complicated. There's a reason that Catholicism has long been the world's preeminent blue-collar Faith. Our churches might look "high class." Our leaders might be brilliant. But our pews have always been filled with average guys like you and me. The

---

[5] John Paul II, Address of the Holy Father John Paul II, August 19, 2000, http://www.vatican.va/content/john-paul-ii/en/speeches/2000/jul-sep/documents/hf_jp-ii_spe_20000819_gmg-veglia.html.

halls of heaven are filled with simple saints. Don't make the mistake of confusing *simple* and *down to earth* with *simplistic* and *inglorious*.

Christianity is simple and glorious all at the same time.

Seek God in daily prayer. Seek him in the sacraments. Seek him in his Word. Seek him in community with other Christians.[6] Seek him by serving the poor—spiritually and materially. Seek him by hanging holy things on your walls.[7] The essence of Christianity is Christ. You'll find him in all those simple ways. And when you have him, you have joy. And the more you do those things, the more you'll create space in your heart for Joy Himself.

---

[6] There are plenty of resources on RealLifeCatholic.com to help you form small group communities.

[7] Check out my sister's icons at elizabethzelasko.com.

Jesus Is the Journey

I am the way. —John 14:6

JESUS

JESUS'S FIRST WORDS to humanity in the Gospel of
John were "What do you seek?" (John 1:38). He saw
two men following him. He turned around, locked eyes
with them—it must have been an awkward moment—
and asked them what they wanted.

He knew the answer. They wanted God. They
wanted love. They wanted *joy*. We all do. And he had
come to deliver.

Realizing that as a teenager changed my life. My
parents dragged me off to a retreat that I did not want
to go on. (I love coerced religious experiences for kids
now!) You know what changed my life on this retreat?
It wasn't the speakers on the stage. It wasn't the band. It

wasn't a particular phrase anyone said. It was the faces of the people in that room. As soon as I looked at them, I realized they had the joy that I had always been looking for and had forgotten.

The first Christians called themselves the living ones, and when I looked at the people at that retreat, I realized that I was dead. All my priorities had been about getting drunk, about using girls. This is as early as seventh and eighth grade. I wanted to be like the rock gods I looked up to, all of them dead inside.

I remember one face in that room in particular. He was in his sixties and praising God. His hands were lifted in the air. We didn't talk, and I don't know who he was. He certainly wasn't "cool" like my rock idols. And he'd never guess that he's a big part of why you're holding this book in your hands. His face showed me that joy wasn't the absence of pain or the presence of some pleasure but was, rather, the presence of God—with all his divine joy—living and laughing within us.

THE JOY OF GOD

Let's think of something mighty: God's mirth.

Think of a joy that wells up from the depths and leads to that bodily convulsion we call laughter. It doesn't come from deep contemplation—just some happy reality bashing into your wide-open soul. A good name for that kind of joy is "mirth."

G. K. Chesterton ended his book *Orthodoxy* with a reflection on the mirth of God that I want to share as I wrap up this book:

And as I close this chaotic volume I open again the strange small book from which all Christianity came; and I am again haunted by a kind of confirmation. The tremendous figure which fills the Gospels towers in this respect, as in every other, above all the thinkers who ever thought themselves tall. His pathos was natural, almost casual. The Stoics, ancient and modern, were proud of concealing their tears. He never concealed His tears; He showed

> "All the way to heaven is heaven, because Jesus said, 'I am the way.'" —Catherine of Siena

them plainly on His open face at any daily sight, such as the far sight of His native city. Yet He concealed something. Solemn supermen and imperial diplomatists are proud of restraining their anger. He never restrained His anger. He flung furniture down the front steps of the Temple, and asked men how they expected to escape the damnation of Hell. Yet He restrained something. I say it with reverence; there was in that shattering personality a thread that must be called shyness. There was something that He hid from all men when He went up a mountain to pray. There was something that He covered constantly by abrupt silence or impetuous isolation. There was some one thing that was too great for God to show us when He walked upon our earth; and I have sometimes fancied that it was His mirth.[1]

---

[1] G. K. Chesterton, *Orthodoxy*, in *The Collected Works of G. K. Chesterton*,

Everything in this book is about tapping into the well-spring of joy, the mirth of God himself! St. Pope John Paul II often expressed that the joy we experience in life reflects the original joy that God felt in creating us. I love to think of the deeply satisfied, gut-level laugh that welled up from the heart of love 13.8 billion years ago and produced a universe—and you. Had Jesus not kept that under wraps, it might have blown up everything. Every taste of pure joy, from the wedding-day smile to the silent satisfaction as you soak in the sound of rain is a foretaste of the joy to come. It's a joy he wants you to have.

BORN AGAIN IN JOY

What you just read is about tapping into the heart of God himself. It's no ordinary "self-help" book. Those can only go so far. There's an old saying that sums many of those books up: *Pull yourself up by the bootstraps.* In other words, "succeed without any outside help." And it's stupid. Think about what that phrase actually means. To reach down, grab your boots, and pull up isn't going to get you *up.* I don't care how much self-reliance and self-confidence you have. I don't care how many self-help books you read.

These rules are about something greater than self-help: God's help. Following these rules merely prepares the way for he who IS joy. And the fact that he lets you cooperate with him in what he wants to do in your life (which is why this book is in your hands) is itself a grace.

vol. 1 (San Francisco, CA: Ignatius, 1986), chap. 9.

This is what no secular motivational speaker, no atheist, no vaguely spiritual person, and no pagan can offer you. But I can. It's Jesus. You can't have fullness of joy without him, because you can't have joy without love, and there is no love that compares with what we find in the God who is love and made us for himself. Sure, you can trip over happy experiences because we have a God who wants to be found and who can't be hidden. But the joy of Paul in prison, John Simone in his hut in Haiti, Chiara Badano on her deathbed, or my dad on his—supernatural joy—is impossible without life in God.

When you are in Christ, you are a new creation, one born again in joy.

That doesn't mean life is easy. "We do not pretend that life is all beauty. We are aware of darkness and sin, of poverty and pain. But . . . we live in the light of his Paschal Mystery . . . 'We are an Easter People and Alleluia is our song!' We are not looking for a shallow joy but rather a joy that comes from faith."[2]

I lost a dear friend ten years ago, and his fourth child was born two weeks after he died. At his funeral, the priest said, "Joy isn't the absence of pain. It's the presence of Jesus."

THE SIMPLE PATH

I hope that many things you've read about living a life of joy made you think, "That's very simple. Stupidly

[2] John Paul II, Angelus, November 30, 1986, no. 3, http://www.vatican.va/content/john-paul-ii/en/angelus/1986/documents/hf_jp-ii_ang_19861130.html.

simple." And I hope that realization makes you realize how stupid it is not to follow these rules! Don't focus on what stands in the way.

When David faced Goliath, he had a big problem standing between him and his destiny. A very big, giant-sized problem. He didn't focus on the problem. He kept his eyes on God. And that brought him to a stunningly simple solution. When Saul tried to bog him down with armor and a sword, it was too clunky for David. No thanks. He dropped it and reached for his sling and five smooth stones.

Many things stand between you and the joy-filled life you were made for. I'm sure many of those things came to mind as you read this book. I hope you don't get caught up in all that, but that you stick to implementing all the practices in this book. They're your sling and smooth stones. And these rules, these smooth stones, are how Jesus lived.

Jesus:

- Gave thanks. (Luke 22:19)
- Retreated to the silence. (Luke 5:16)
- Loved himself, because we know he always practiced what he preached we should do. (Matt 22:39)
- Had fun. He walked on water alone at night (John 6:19 . . . don't tell me that wasn't fun!) and celebrated and feasted with people (Matt 11:19; John 2:1–12).
- Was physically active. He walked thousands of miles during his public ministry, with each round trip from Galilee to Jerusalem alone—and he made many—being over 150 miles.
- Had friends. (John 15:15)

- Rested. (Mark 6:31)
- Served. (John 13:5)
- And always kept his eyes on the Father. (Luke 23:46)

His path was one of joy. And when we walk with him, we discover living joy, even when our way is the cross.

CLOSE

Let's finish where we started. Dad. Heart attack. ICU. My mother sitting in quiet and looking at her beloved after almost fifty years of marriage.

I could see profound pain in my mom's face in those moments. Her sadness was real. She wasn't in denial of the gravity of her situation. She was saying goodbye. But something else was present and was *more* real: Christian joy, anchored in her hope of eternal love. Heaven is no less real than your pain. Nor is it ever far off. "The kingdom of heaven is at hand" (Matt 3:2). Always. That is the "light [that] shines in the darkness, and the darkness has not overcome it" (John 1:5). And that is why joy was her strength and gratitude was her prayer, even then.

Someday, when I'm long gone, my son will be in a hospital bed as an old man with his wife and his son by his side. I hope he's experienced many of life's blessings by then. I hope he's had a good job, beautiful and healthy children who honor him, and a great marriage, but above all, I hope that he finds his strength in the joy of the Lord as his grandparents did. Even then.

I'd like for you to have an easy life, but more, I wish you Jesus, my friend, because I wish you joy.

Thank you for taking this journey with me. Stay on it. Walk this simple path with the Lord. These nine rules for life aren't a sprint but a marathon. I'm praying for you. I'll always be praying for those who read this book. So will my team of prayer warriors and Carmelite nuns whom I've asked to lift you up in prayer while you read. I'm not giving up on you. Don't you give up on you.

> "Joy is the keynote of the Christian message." —John Paul II

I echo down the words of Nehemiah to you today. The city walls have been torn down. Raiders surround us on every side. Pandemics and crazy political movements threaten you every time you open your door. Will you become angry, or let your heart be torn down? God is calling you to battle. He's calling you to rebuild your fallen city, your Church, your family, and the world. This is his battle cry for you today.

When you live in joy, you have Godlike strength for every decision you make, every encounter you have, and every battle you face in life. The call is urgent, and it's not just about you. The world needs you. The Church needs you. Your family and friends need you. Teenage me (dragged to a religious retreat against his will) needs to see your joy: "The joy of the Lord MUST be your strength" (see Neh 8:10).

We are writing this that our joy may be complete. (1 John 1:4)

John Paul II's Angelus During His Visit to Australia, November 30, 1986

At the end of this Eucharistic celebration, I invite you to join me in praying the Angelus. This prayer takes its name from the Angel's message to Mary: "Rejoice . . . the Lord is with you." Soon, in the Christmas liturgy, you will hear those other words of joy which announced the birth of Jesus: "Listen, I bring you news of great joy, a joy to be shared by all the people."

I have said before on another occasion: "In a true sense, joy is the keynote of the Christian message." As I said then, my wish is that the Christian message may bring joy to all who open their hearts to it: "joy to children, joy to parents, joy to families and to friends, joy to workers and scholars, joy to the sick and to the elderly, joy to all humanity." . . .

Faith is our source of joy. We believe in a God who created us so that we might enjoy human happiness—in some measure on earth, in its fullness in heaven. We are meant to have our human joys: the joy of living, the joy of love and friendship, the joy of work well done. We who are Christians have a further cause for joy: like Jesus, we know that we are loved by God our Father. This love transforms our lives and fills us with joy. It makes us see that Jesus did not come to lay burdens upon us. He came to teach us what it means to be fully happy and fully human. Therefore, we discover joy when we discover truth—the truth about God our Father, the truth about Jesus our Saviour, the truth about the Holy Spirit who lives in our hearts.

We do not pretend that life is all beauty. We are aware of darkness and sin, of poverty and pain. But we know Jesus has conquered sin and passed through his own pain to the glory of the Resurrection. And we live in the light of his Paschal Mystery—the mystery of his Death and Resurrection. "We are an Easter People and Alleluia is our song!" We are not looking for a shallow joy but rather a joy that comes from faith, that grows through unselfish love, that respects the "fundamental duty of love of neighbour, without which it would be unbecoming to speak of Joy." We realize that joy is demanding; it demands unselfishness; it demands a readiness to say with Mary: "Be it done unto me according to thy word."

Mary, our Mother: I turn to you and with the Church I invoke you as Mother of Joy (Mater plena sanctae laetitiae). I, John Paul II, entrust to you the Church in Australia, and ask you to pour out upon all her members that holy human joy which was God's gift to you.

Help all your children to see that the good things in their lives come to them from God the Father through your Son Jesus Christ. Help them to experience in the Holy Spirit the joy which filled your own Immaculate Heart. And in the midst of the sufferings and trials of life may they find the fullness of joy that belongs to the victory of your Crucified Son, and comes forth from his Sacred Heart.

Scan this code or go to **reallifecatholic.com/living-joy** for a video version of this book with small group guides!